In this witty and delightful book, Walter Bryan considers the background and temperament of the Irish people, their traditions, their heroes and heroines, their folklore, customs and religion (from St. Patrick to the reactions to the Pope's Encyclical on birth control).

Here you will meet an unforgettable array of Irishmen: Brian Boru, the almost legendary Irish king who was a direct ancestor of the Kennedys; Captain Boycott, whose name added a word to the English language; Sir Boyle Roche, whose undisciplined speeches brightened many a sitting of Irish Parliament ("The cup of Ireland's misfortunes has been overflowing for centuries, and it is not full yet," he warned); Charles Stewart Parnell, the great Irish patriotic leader, condemned by the priesthood, whose funeral in Dublin drew 160,000 mourners; and innumerable others, all very real, and all very, very Irish.

THE IMPROBABLE IRISH is a book you will want to reread and savor many times, whether or not your people are from the Ould Sod.

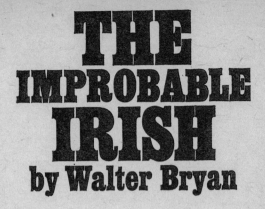

THE IMPROBABLE IRISH
by Walter Bryan

ACE BOOKS, INC.
1120 Avenue of the Americas
New York, N.Y. 10036

THE IMPROBABLE IRISH

AUTHOR'S ACKNOWLEDGMENTS:

To The Clarendon Press, for permission to quote from *The Lore and Language of Schoolchildren* by Iona and Peter Opie.

To Mr. Diarmuid Russell, for permission to quote the lines by George Russell on page 223.

CONTENTS

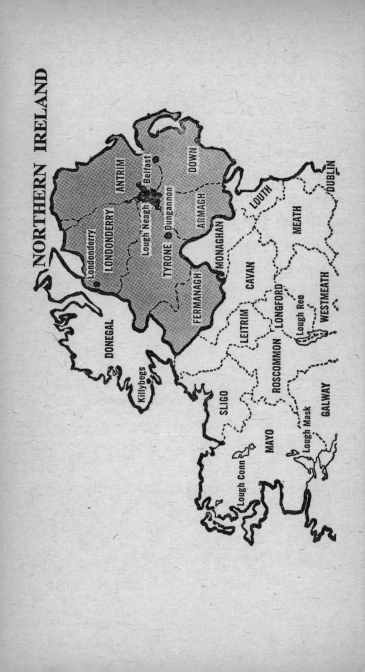

To Charles Harris,
my best friend and severest
critic (alternately)

1. The Glocca Morra Situation

I think it is time the American public had answers to some of the questions which have been posed continually, first over their radio by Bing Crosby and currently by Petula Clark in the movie version of *Finian's Rainbow*. Such as how things are in Glocca Morra.

I can only assume the reason nobody has attempted to answer this question before is that it has not been addressed to the correct quarter. Mr. Crosby and Miss Clark first ask a bird from Londonderry, which is 250 miles away from Glocca Morra as the crow flies; they then interrogate a River Shannon breeze, which is still nearly a hundred miles off course. Glocca Morra is a remote spot in Kerry and one can only assume that if the writer of the song ever traveled there he fell into the hands of an unusually unscrupulous cab driver. However, I have made the journey specially on your account, taking only my wife, family, car, baggage and the advance on this book, and here is a situation report from your Man in Glocca Morra.

Q. *Is that little brook still leaping there?*
A. Yes, I am relieved to report that this is indeed the case. Since it is only about two feet wide the danger of its being harnessed for hydroelectric power was never very great.

Q. *Does it still run down to Donnycove, through Killybegs, Kilkerry and Kildare?*

A. Frankly no, and I am surprised to learn that it ever did, no matter how acrobatic it was. Killybegs is more than two hundred miles to the north and Kildare a hundred miles to the west, which you must admit is quite a startling series of leaps for a little brook to make, especially when you think of all the intervening mountain ranges. As for Donnycove, I am sorry to say I was not able to find this place at all in the *Topographical Dictionary* or *Townland Index of Ireland,* which together contain about a hundred thousand Irish place names, including such unlikely ones as Dirtystep, Bootown and Ballywatticock. Nor could I find anything remotely like it, though I assumed that even an author with the fine old Irish name of E. Y. Harburg might have been forced to make a few changes in the interests of euphony. It was obvious, for instance, that Glocca Morra was originally Glash na Gloragh (the voiceful brook), which I admit cannot be quite as easy to croon into a microphone.

Q. *Is that willow tree still weeping there?*

A. I did not find any willow tree available for interview, and was reluctant to intrude on private grief.

Q. *Does that lassie with the twinkling eye come smiling by?*

A. Not while I was there. Perhaps I shouldn't have brought my wife with me.

Q. *Then does she walk away, sad and dreamy there, not to see me there?*

A.   Presumably. I only hope she doesn't go to look for you in Donnycove.

Q.   *How are Things in Glocca Morra?*
A.   Actually there are very few Things in Glash na Gloragh, but what there are seem in reasonably good condition considering that they have been lying out in the rain so long. The rocks show signs of wear, but the grass and heather appear to have recently been renewed.

Before we leave the Glocca Morra area, there is a real estate problem in that neighborhood which used to concern singers almost as much.

Q.   *How can you buy Killarney?*
A.   The answer to this really depends on how much of it you want. If you would be satisfied with part of it, the first thing to do is to write to a reputable estate agent in the locality. Plots of ground in Killarney Urban District are sold locally at less than $1500 an acre, but fetch more than twice that when sold through advertisements in foreign newspapers. There might also be tax to pay because the Irish are getting worried about how, after fighting foreigners seven hundred years for their country, another lot are now buying it from under them.

If however you want to purchase the Killarney Estate itself, I am afraid you are too late. It was bought in 1959 by an American, Mr. John McShain, and I don't think he has any intention of disposing of it. To his eternal credit he has thrown it open to the public free of charge. The rest of the scenic district known as Killarney is owned by the Irish Government as a National Park, having been presented to Ireland by some even more generous Americans, Mr. and Mrs. Bourn of California and Mr. Arthur Vincent. May their shadow never grow less. I can see very little prospect of the Irish Government selling it to you, even if you bought Northern Ireland and offered it in exchange. An eccentric American millionaire did once attempt to solve the Partition problem by offering to buy Northern Ireland, but the British Government was not interested and could certainly not have offered possession.

In any event, solutions to problems in Ireland are never as simple as that. As Ed Murrow once said about Vietnam, anyone who isn't confused doesn't really understand the situation.

There is, it seems to me, confusion even about songs such as those I have just quoted. Many people in Ireland feel a great hatred for songs like these, which are obviously written by people who know nothing about Ireland, just to make money. I shared that hatred myself, until one day I lost it in a supermarket. I had strayed into the unfamiliar regions of the cereals department and there, among the alien corn, the truth dawned on me.

In the British Isles a rather touching relationship has grown up in the last fifty years or so between suburban housewives and wild birds. It has become the custom for the average suburban housewife to throw out her food scraps on the lawn for the birds and watch them while she washes the dishes, and they become her friends in the lonely mornings. In coastal districts housewives attend courses on how to clean seabirds being killed by oil pollution on their wings. The average housewife knows

14

that many wild birds have by now become completely dependent on people like her, and in wintertime when there are not enough scraps for them she throws out fresh bread. The cereal manufacturers observed the phenomenon, realized the need and now market under the trade name SWOOP a balanced diet for wild birds.

It appears to sell well, which is a tribute to the kindness of thousands of ordinary women. It seems to me it is a credit to the manufacturers too that they should help the women give effect to their good intentions, even if they make money out of it, and that the same credit might be given to the writers of fake Irish songs. If many ordinary people feel an affection for and an interest in Ireland, and for some reason they do, surely it is a good thing that they should be given a way to express it. The affection might occasionally be misguided and the interest ill-informed, but the birds do not complain that the housewives who love them are not ornithologists.

However, the Irish are more than wild creatures who have had a hard time, and sing prettily, and have never done anyone any harm. For all the number of them, they and their tiny island have made a great stir in the world, and it is well worth anyone's time to find out more about them and the country which made them.

2. How to Tell an Irishman

If you meet a man in a bar and he offers you shares in a shamrock quarry in his peat bog in Londonderry, view him with the utmost suspicion. Peat is called turf in Ireland and Derry is called Derry, as it was before James I sold it to some London merchants in 1613. This character does not come from Ireland, whatever might be said about his old wire-haired mother.

Fortunately you could assess his credentials even without having obscure information like this, because the national characteristics of the Irish are very well known. Perhaps it would be a help if I were to just set them out to remind you, adding any additional information that might be of interest.

The Irish are drunks. It is said that the Eskimos have eleven different words for snow, and no doubt it is for similar reasons that the Irish have at least as many synonyms for intoxication. (Full, cut, stoven, sozzled, maggoty, stoned, blithero, stotious, half tore, blind, and blutered in Belfast or fluthered in Dublin.) So there is no doubt that a lot of Irishmen like a drink now and then and it is socially acceptable in most of Ireland. For instance blood donors, who are of course unpaid, get a glass of Guinness afterwards: in the North it's a cup of tea. It is also true that some of them drink too much, filling the alcoholic wards and fooling some statisticians. But other statisticians note that the per capita consumption of whiskey in Ireland is less than in Scotland, and of beer etc. less than in England.

I think I can hear someone jeering that no doubt they also drink less tequila than the Mexicans, with the insinuation that they are filling up on poteen while the statisticians' backs are turned. In fact many Irishmen have never even seen poteen (pronounced pot-yeen by the Irish and poison by the medical profession) and most know better than to drink it when they do. Poteen making is a dying craft, like its customers. The only man I ever heard of who made any money out of it did it by buying war surplus distillation equipment by mail at ten pounds a set and concealing it about the bogs; he then informed on these illicit stills to another department of the British Government, receiving twenty pounds reward for each.

Many Irishmen used to drink too much, at a time when it was the only alternative to suicide, and their present reputation is a sort of hangover from then. One wonders which of the other nations who are pointing those rather unsteady fingers of scorn have not had similar periods in their own history, with far less excuse for them. I seem to remember that it was not so long ago that the staid English were patronizing gin palaces offering to make them drunk for a penny and dead drunk for twopence, with straw for sleeping it off on a halfpenny extra.

The Irish are priest-ridden. Those Irish who are Catholics are certainly very devoted to their Church, especially since the English tried to suppress it, and will defend it against all comers. Among themselves however they regretfully recognize it as composed of fallible human beings. As the Irish barrister Paddy Kelly is said to have put it, "The Irish Bishops are individually virtuous and sapient men, wise in precept and impeccable in practise. But it is a great misfortune that they should always fix their meetings for an occasion when the Holy Ghost happens to be engaged elsewhere."

It is also a strange thing in a priest-ridden country that every national leader in its long struggle for independence should have been a Protestant, with the single exception of De Valera, and he was excommunicated without apparent effect. And that the Irish have been known to disobey a clear and direct instruction from the Pope on a matter of morals when they didn't want to stop what they were doing. Their ingenious technique for dismantling unexploded Papal Encyclicals (Chapter 14) should be of considerable interest nowadays.

Incidentally, the song "Father O'Flynn" was written by a Protestant.

The Irish are pugnacious and violent. This is as true as it was of the French naturalist's famous description of a wild animal: "This creature is very vicious. When attacked it defends itself." No doubt it is only because the Irish have been so busy doing this that they have never attacked another country or persecuted a racial minority. (Ireland did not even take part in the Crusades, much to the annoyance of the Pope.) But it does seem strange that even during the most troublous times of her history the incidence of violent crimes was always so much less than in England; and that I should have survived several long hot summers in Ireland, not to mention some thirty short wet ones, without ever having seen one adult strike another in anger except on English television.

The Irish are sentimental and impractical. No. Here for once I'm afraid I'll have to disagree. The Irish are hard-headed, even cynical. The only sentimental things about them are fake Irish songs like "Mother Machree," which no Irishman would be heard dead singing. The real Irish song is more like that cheerful marching tune in which a girl greets her wounded lover home from the wars, with increasingly macabre verses ending:

> *You haven't an arm and you haven't a leg.*
> *You're an eyeless, noseless, chickenless egg.*
> *You'll have to be put with a bowl to beg.*
> *Johnny, I hardly knew you.*

The Irish have no illusions about war, and their proverbs indicate none about ordinary life. "Death is the poor man's doctor." "If you want praise, die; if you want blame, marry." In the industrial North, where they are if possible even more down to earth and practical, they have a saying which tells more about human nature than I think I really want to know: "A borrowed saw cuts anything."

In early Irish versions of the Scriptures, David did not go to fight Goliath on a mere promise: he demanded and received sureties from Saul that his reward would be forthcoming when he won, a sensible precaution the Irish assumed he would have taken. The English novelist Anthony Trollope, who lived for some time in Ireland, wrote:

> *I found them to be good-humored, clever—the*
> *working classes much more intelligent than those*

of England—economical and hospitable. We hear much of their spendthrift nature; but extravagance is not the nature of an Irishman. He will count the shillings in a pound much more accurately than an Englishman and will with much more certainty get twelve pennyworth from each.

When Parnell, the famous patriotic leader, was arrested in 1881 at the Morrison Hotel in Dublin the proprietor offered him an escape route out the back; however the great man preferred to accept his imprisonment with dignity and accompanied the police without resistance. But on the way out the martyred hero paused to haggle over his hotel bill. I do not say that Parnell was a typical Irishman, but I do adduce in evidence a Dublin street ballad which was popular soon after and included among its tributes to their champion the following admiring verse:

> They took him and they bound him, them minions
> of the Law.
> 'Twas Pat the Boots was there that night and told
> me all he saw.
> But sorra a step the patriot bold would leave the place
> until
> They granted him a ten percent reduction on his bill.

Lady Fingall in her autobiography describes a more embarrassing scene at a French hotel, where a sum was added to their hotel bill for a broken bedroom utensil. Her husband stormed upstairs and came down carrying the chamber pot, swearing that if he had to pay for it he was going to take it with him.

Among the many stories which are supposed to illustrate the impracticality and foolishness of the Irish, like the one about the level crossing keeper who left his gates half open because he was half expecting a train, I know of only one that is authentic. This concerned the three young children of Richard Littledale, a 19th Century barrister. They had saved up their pocket money to buy their father a present and had accumulated the vast sum of three shillings, with which they proposed to buy him a red kerchief. They found just what they wanted in a shop, but it turned out to be two shillings and eleven pence, which is not divisible by three. Fortunately the eldest child almost immediately saw the solution to the problem. "Make it three shillings and we'll take it."

Stories making the Irish out to be overgrown infants became popular because for a long time it suited the English to think of them in this way. For the same reason such stories are now told by white couples in bars in South Africa to illustrate to visitors how completely irresponsible and untrustworthy the colored people are, a flow of anecdote which can only momentarily be arrested by asking who is looking after the children.

The Irish are to blame for their reputation too, because some of them retell these stories themselves and others even act them out for the benefit of strangers. One of the great Irish faults is that they never can resist a joke, a failing which lands them in endless trouble. I have heard of a Dublin lawyer who, on visits to London for the rugby internationals, was in the habit of amusing himself and his friends by lurching up to policemen with his cap pulled over his eyes and asking, "I beg your pardon, Sor, are there any moving pictures in this town?" Whatever the answer he would stagger away exclaiming

"Faith and begorrah!"—the only time he ever used the expressions in his life.

In the same way, if a visitor to Ireland happens to be the sort of person who throws his weight about, he will come home with enough stories of Irish incompetence to last him a lifetime. Jonah Barrington saw through this as early as 1803 when he wrote: "The sharpest wit and the shrewdest subtlety which abound in the character of the Irish peasant generally lie concealed under the appearance of simplicity."

On the other hand, if you are a decent sort of fellow, and the Irish will always give a stranger the benefit of the doubt, they will go to immense trouble so that you will not be disappointed. They feel personally responsible for everything in Ireland that might affect your holiday, even the weather: if you say it is a fine day they glow with pride, and if you complain about the rain they feel guilty about it and make lame excuses about it being good for the fishing. So it is not surprising that they try to make such other improvements in the local situations as lie within their power.

For instance I used to think of Belfast as an ordinary modern industrial city until one day I escorted an American girl fom the airport terminal to the main railroad station. I found her deep in conversation with a porter who had carried her baggage out to the street, had refused a tip and wished her a pleasant holiday, and was now halfway through planning an itinerary for her. The cab driver stopped his meter to detour through the more pleasant parts of the town pointing out places of interest, like the Titanic Memorial. Outside the railroad station a Character materialized from the sidewalk, the like of whom I had never seen in my life, asked her what part of the States she was from, invited her to look up his relatives there, and disappeared again with a most charmingly turned compliment. Inside the station the train from force of habit started dead on time, but saved the day by stopping again halfway out to let on an old lady who had arrived late. The city of Belfast then heaved a little sigh and went back to making money, but it never seemed quite the same to me again.

The fact is that everyone gets the Irish he deserves.

Their hospitality has given the Irish their reputation for extravagance, and more than once done them great harm. In 1541, in a time of war and poverty, an English visitor wrote, "Though they never did see you before they will make you the best cheer their country yieldeth for two or three days and take not anything therefor," and reported meals of milk, butter, herbs, spices, swans, partridge, plovers, quails, oysters, salmon, ale, mead, nectar and whiskey. What once aroused greed later justified apathy. In 1830 a Royal Commission reported that Irish farmers gave away a million pounds worth of food every year to the poor, a fact which convinced the English that there was plenty of food in the country. They refused to believe the Irish when they claimed to be starving until with characteristic perverseness they started dying like flies.

I suppose you will by now have quite given up hope of being reassured that all Irishmen have red hair and are called O'Something. I am afraid that all I can offer along these lines is the information that the majority of Irish people are of Blood Group O (indicative of Nordic ancestry). However, my barber tells me that quite a number of Irishmen are red-headed, about one in a hundred; and there are twenty-two pages of O'Somethings in the Dublin telephone directory. There are also twenty pages of McOthers, but both are outnumbered by English names. This is partly because through the centuries many Irish families changed their names to escape persecution or evade discrimination, often simply by translating them into English. The Sinnachs became Foxes, the Mac-anghobhanns Smiths, the Galbhains Whites, the Brannachs Walshes. The state of the Dublin telephone directory though may largely be accounted for by an edict of Edward IV in 1464 that "all residing within the counties of Meath, Dublin and Kildare should adopt an English surname—either from a town, or from some color, or some trade or office; and their posterity should retain that name in future time." So even if your name is Sutton or Chester or Black or Brown or Taylor or Carpenter or Cook or Butler, you may still be descended from the High Kings of Ireland.

However, being Irish is not a matter of parentage. It is an infectious condition endemic in the region, against which there is no protection but complete isolation, and for which there is no cure but death. As the wife of an English Prime Minister once said sadly, "Ireland is a country one comes to love like a person." So all the people who have come to Ireland and fallen in love with it, Norse and Norman and English, are now as much Irish as anyone if not more so. "It is not a question of race," said George Moore, "it is the land itself that makes the Celt."

"This has never been a rich or powerful country," said John Kennedy, "and yet, since earliest times, its influence on the world has been rich and powerful. . . . No larger nation did more to spark the cause of independence in America, indeed round the world. And no other nation has ever provided the world with more literary and artistic genius. This is an extraordinary country. . . ."

3. The Utmost Corner of the West

I have often thought that the authorities at Shannon Airport should provide a small patch of grass in the middle of the aerodrome for returning exiles to fall on and kiss. Few people perform this ritual on the tarmac, except perhaps with the unexpected assistance of a patch of oil, and an emotional need remains unfulfilled. For there is no other moment as sharply defined as that first step on Irish ground: the Irishness of Ireland is a thing of subtlety and soft light, and even the transition to it from the airport's Standard International Environment is a gradual one.

A noisy transatlantic bustle seeps from the airport, contaminating the countryside for several miles in every direction. The nearest picturesque ruin, Bunratty Castle, has been restored and refurbished at great expense and provides the latest in tape-recorded commentaries and in 16th Century banquets at 20th Century prices. You can taste syllabub and venison, and learn that halfway through the castle's history it was successfully defended by one Admiral Penn, whose young son, not to be outdone, promptly went and founded Pennsylvania. But while it may be interesting to speculate where Pittsburg would be if those walls had been a foot less thick, you came all this way to learn about Ireland. And while the castle has been restored with exquisite taste it is not, for better or for worse, typical of Ireland. The typical Irish castle is hidden away down a leafy lane and always comes as such a surprise that ever afterwards you secretly feel it is your very own ruined castle. And indeed it may well be, for nobody else seems to own them and there are enough to go around.

So my advice would be to browse around for your own castle. There are 189 of them in this little county of Clare alone, together with 2,300 forts, 130 prehistoric tombs, 150 ancient churches, three cathedrals, eight monasteries, five round towers and ten stone crosses. They were counted by a man called Westropp, who seems to have been an archaeologist with insomnia. This is the county of the O'Briens and the McNamaras and the Quinns, and before that of Brian Boru, forefather of the Kennedys. It has not always been appreciated by foreigners, the most notorious critical review having come from an English gentleman who accompanied Cromwell on his memorable tour of Ireland. He complained that in the northern part of it there was "not a tree to hang a man, no water in which to drown him, no soil in which to bury him." The deficiencies of their county had not struck its inhabitants in just that way before and they were so loathe to leave it that the English just had to do the best they could with their available resources to meet their simple needs.

They succeeded so well that to this day England is to the people of these parts a more remote and hostile place than America. An old Clare woman I heard of, asked where her sons were, said, "Two of them are in

26

America, and one away in England." Emigration may be a sort of death to the Irish—there is a ceremony in the countryside called an "American Wake"—but while America is something like heaven to them, England has many of the attributes of hell. Brendan Behan used to tell a story about a priest who fulminated every Sunday from his pulpit about the wickedness of the English, until the Bishop told him to stop it. He was not to mention the English again. So next Sunday the priest announced that his subject was the Last Supper, and went on with a graphic account of the events of that evening, climaxing with: "And the Lord said to his Apostles, 'One of you will betray me,' and his eye lit on Judas. And Judas sprang guiltily to his feet, crying: 'Cor blimey, guv, turn it up.'"

Retracing the glide path of your aeroplane would take you through Ennis, where during the Troubles of the twenties De Valera was arrested while making a speech. Released some months later he went back to Ennis, mounted the same rostrum and continued, "As I was saying when I was interrupted . . ." Then along the green banks of Spenser's "spacious Shannon spreading like the sea" to the seaside resort of Kilkee. This is the holiday place of everyone's childhood, complete with little golden waves and sandcastles, and the promenade steps where you scraped your toe, and the rows of boarding house porches filled with gaily colored buckets and wooden spades. It fulfills even the impossible dreams of children, for every now and then one of them finds in the sand a golden doubloon washed up from the wrecks of the Spanish Armada that lie off Spanish Point. It is there that the road leaves the sea, rather than disturb the little coves and tiny villages where the same families come year after year without telling anyone else about them, only to return to it with a great flourish of golden sands at Lahinch. Behind the sands are great dunes among which lurks a fearsome golf course, for men with iron nerves and bags full of old balls. You could dream a day away among the wild flowers in these sunny hollows, where every prospect pleases and only Man shouts "Fore," but you would get more peace in the overgrown cuttings of the famous West Clare Railway. There now are only the happy memories of thousands of children who came on this railroad to Kilkee, and here first saw the sea. One of them was called Kate O'Brien, and she became a very great writer in the world without ever forgetting that moment. Nowadays in Ireland children go to the seaside every weekend in the family car, and I suppose that is better, but I cannot help wishing they could also have that first piercing moment of joy at the first sight of the sea from the train. But for every happy memory the abandoned railway now offers a wild strawberry, so many that you can nibble all afternoon and save enough to have with fresh cream after dinner.

If you could bear to leave Lahinch and continue north you would enter a black and sinister world of dark cliffs and maddened seas. These are the Cliffs of Moher, the Great Wall of Thomond, a fitting climax to the continent of Europe. Here you can drop a stone seven hundred feet into the foam—on a calm day; on a windy one you can see it stop in mid-air and fly back over your head. On these cliffs you can stalk along over the Atlantic for miles to the hidden bay of Doolin, a wild and lonely place of white sand and towering cliffs and tormented waves. Then suddenly you are in the Burren, the place that Cromwell's friend found so inadequate. Naturalists could spend their lives there nonetheless, because it is a huge natural rock garden where they find even the rarest Arctic and Alpine plants. And one Sunday morning a young man walking his dog found there the Golden Gorget of Gillasheen where it had lain undisturbed for over a thousand years, as exquisite as the day the neckband was made. But anything can happen in this mysterious limestone desert, where rivers disappear into vast unexplored caverns, and where the sea mysteriously fills the countless circular basins in the great flat slabs that shelve its shore.

Four miles inland is the ghost town of Lisdoonvarna. In the 19th Century it was the most famous spa in Ireland, and people flocked to it in such numbers that on Sundays the churches had to hold masses in the open air. Then people lost their faith in the magic secular waters, and Lisdoonvarna began to die. The town still has a lively social life in the summer, but the great pump rooms which were its heart are in slow and remorseless decay. Something I found there made them seem to me a peculiarly Irish type of ruin.

After some time in Ireland one becomes quite a connoisseur of ruins. The ruin is virtually an Irish art form, and certainly its premier architectural feature. No doubt the number of them is mainly due to the troubled history of the country, but the extravagance of the national character must have something to do with it. In England when a building is in danger of becoming dilapidated, each generation patches it up with loving care, until in time it becomes a sort of anthology of architecture through the ages. In America before a building has a chance to look dilapidated, they tear it down and build something bigger. But in Ireland buildings are just allowed to get more and more dilapidated until they fall down, whereupon the Irish build another one further down the road.

Whatever the reason, Ireland sometimes seems to have more accommodation for ghosts than for people. First there are all those prehistoric tombs and burial mounds; then the thousands of castles and forts where the Norse, the Normans, the English and the natives defended themselves against each other; and then all the churches and cathedrals that were burned down when their custodians picked the wrong side to declare that God was on. Like the Great Cathedral of Cashel, burned down by the Earl of Kildare: taxed afterwards with this wanton act he said he was sorry, but he'd thought the Archbishop was inside. Next came the Famine and the evictions, when half the population died or went to America—if you have an Irish name it is very likely that your ancestral home is still standing, with a fine crop of nettles growing in the living room. Then there were the Troubles of the twenties, when the people got their revenge for the evictions by burning down the stately homes of the now crash-landed gentry. Since then things have been unnaturally quiet, except for the continuing effects of an Irish phenomenon which you might call Unplanned Obsolescence. By the time any technological innovation reaches Ireland, it is apt to be on its way out everywhere else. While the Irish were furiously building railroads, for instance, the English and Americans were sneakily inventing the motor car, and there came a time when railroad lines were being closed before they were opened.

These were almost what one might call purpose-built ruins.

There is even a small category of what might be described as ruined ruins. In the latter part of the 19th Century an English archaeologist found an interesting ruined castle on the outskirts of Belfast. He thought it was important to preserve what was left of it, which was not very much, so he arranged with a local builder to construct a wall around the site, and went back to England. Some months later he got the bill for the wall and in sending the check remarked pleasantly that it was less than he had expected. The contractor, sending his receipt, explained that he had been able to save money by using a lot of old stones he had found in the middle of the field. . . .

But as I was saying about the ruin in Lisdoonvarna: amid the marbled splendor and convoluted brass plumbing of the Pump Room, made to last a thousand years, is this map showing the attractions of the Spa in its golden age. It shows a complex system of paths linking arbours, aviaries, croquet lawns, fountains, Japanese gardens, river walks and many other Victorian delights. So impressed was I with the grandeur of it all that I went to look for the remains of the splendor that had been Lisdoonvarna, but after fighting my way through dense undergrowth for half an hour found nothing more remarkable than an old man scything a fairway for what was presumably intended to be a pitch-and-putt golf course. After the customary pleasantries I indicated our surroundings and ventured a few philosophic observations on the ravages of time and the vanity of human endeavor. He courteously implied that I attached too much importance to a ninepenny pitch-and-putt course. Eventually it became clear that none of the marvels shown on that map had ever existed. It was not the map of a real place, but the map of a dream. This was what Lisdoonvarna had meant to make of itself had its prosperity continued. All ruins are sad, but there is some happiness in them, for they have lived their lives and served their purpose. The same cannot be said of the ruin of a dream, and there are many such in Ireland.

But perhaps I should discontinue this travelogue here, and point out that Lisdoonvarna is only twenty miles from Shannon Airport, and yet we have seen river and mountain, cliff and strand, meadowland and desert, moorland and parkland, cavern and castle, past and present, and still seen only a small part of the one county of Clare; and not even its historic Limerick, city of Lola Montez and the Broken Treaty and the Wild Geese. To be able to see a continent in a county, eight thousand years of history in a few acres, that is the first fascination of Ireland.

The Eurasian continent is dominated by two great mountain chains, one running down through Scandinavia and the other up through the Carpathians, Alps and Pyrenees. These two world structural lines converge in Ireland, before disappearing beneath the Atlantic and appearing briefly again crossed over in the confusion of the Appalachians. Europe is thus a wedge projecting into the Atlantic, and Ireland is its apex. Everything in Europe focuses to a point in this little island, its bewildering variety of scenery distilled into this jewel on the blue velvet of the Atlantic like a gift to the New World. In North Donegal, in the latitude of Labrador, one can stand on the shore of a fjord at midnight and still see clearly the seals playing in the breakers rolling in from Iceland. While in Kerry, only three hundred miles to the south, palm trees and West Indian plants flourish in the sub-tropical air of the Gulf Stream. In between are dream memories of all the European landscapes: the Sierras of Tipperary, the Massif of the Mournes, even the volcanic peaks of Errigal.

Here are the people of Europe too, and all the sadness and glory of their history, because this tiny island has always been the last refuge for the hunted and the last stand of lost causes. In language, religion, art and history it knits together the strands of European civilization, and once it saved the soul of that civilization during a long European night, and may do so again. But while it is the quintessence of the Old World, and its bridge with the New, it is also uniquely and magically itself, like no other country in the world.

4. Firbolgs, Fomorians and Fairies

Ireland came into existence quite suddenly one day about eight thousand years ago, and was promptly populated by refugees from floods in China. This is the sort of firm courageous statement you can hardly get from a historian these days, but it is not very far from the truth.

Towards the end of the last Ice Age there was a great westward movement of people going on, one of the great mass migrations which have been the groundswell beneath the waves of history. Sometimes one of these great convulsions is analyzed, as when Gibbon traced the connection between the rise of the Han Dynasty in China and the arrival of half a million Mongolians on the shores of the Danube, but throughout the history of Man the great heart of Asia has been pumping new blood to every extremity of the world. It seems plausible that the melting glaciers flooding the populous lowlands of China must have caused such a convulsion, though there were no historians to record it, and all the archaeologists can tell us is that people from Asia were moving into Europe.

They were slightly more advanced than the Europeans, using their stone implements for farming rather than hunting. What followed was rather like the conflict between the homesteaders and the ranchers in the American West, and it resulted in the hunters retreating into the north and west of Europe, now being released by the glaciers and reawakening to life.

By about 6000 B.C. some of them had reached Scotland, which was in those times still attached to Ireland by a narrow land bridge. But the glaciers were melting faster and faster, the level of the sea was rising rapidly, and one day the tide flowed over the land bridge and did not recede. Ireland had become an island and started its independent existence.

The first prehistoric settlements in Ireland have been traced to Counties Antrim and Down, which are only a few miles from Scotland, and it seems plausible that they were founded by some adventurous hunters cut off by the tide. These first involuntary Irishmen found themselves surrounded by thick forests of pine and oak, through which great rivers of melting ice ran into vast marshes, and where roamed packs of wolves and wild boar. There may also have been an occasional Irish elk left over from the days when the country was semi-Arctic, and resolving to become extinct at the first available opportunity. A dense forest is no place for a creature with a fourteen foot span of antlers.

Altogether it must have been a more spectacular landscape than it is now, but much less pleasant to look at or live in. Nowadays in Ireland everywhere there are great vistas of green slopes and blue hills which lead the eye and the mind eagerly over the horizon, whereas thickly wooded country is cloistered and confining. Walking in thick forest has always seemed to me like being in a very healthy subway.

But the air was warm, this being the beginning of the great Atlantic Climactic period, which was to last three thousand years. The sea teemed with unsophisticated fish, the shores were festooned with succulent bivalves, and the colonies survived. According to the archaeologists nothing else very dramatic happened, except that more settlers arrived by boat and joined in the routine progression through the use of copper and bronze to iron, as was then the fashion everywhere else in Europe.

Fortunately we know from generations of children, who remembered the stories told them by their grandfathers well enough to pass them on to their grandchildren, that a great many more extraordinary things did happen than people just making a great many cooking pots and arrowheads. For example, the first person ever to arrive in Ireland was a girl called Cesair, who was a granddaughter of Noah. She had come there because it was already well known that Ireland had no snakes, and she thought it might escape the Deluge on that account.

Apparently her reasoning was that the whole unfortunate situation had been brought about by that snake in the Garden of Eden, and the absence of reptiles from Ireland might mean that the country was another Eden, free from sin, at the opposite corner of the known world. Unfortunately this is not the case, despite all appearances to the contrary, and this early example of feminine intuition proved to be misguided. Cesair was drowned, along with the fifty maidens and three men she had brought with her. A man called Finntann was, however, miraculously revived and made immortal, charged with the eternal duty of wandering about the country warning people not to be too smug about being in Ireland. The Irish Tourist Board has him chained up in the basement of its Dublin office.

Next there came the followers of a man called Neimheadh, who settled down peacefully for quite a while until they were attacked by a mysterious race from under the sea called the Fomorians. These were not a prepossessing lot by all accounts, having only one eye and one arm. They were led by a fierce woman who had four eyes in her back, a useful attribute for any unpopular leader. Fed up with the Fomorians, the descendants of Neimheadh up and left the country and went to Greece, where they were sold into slavery and spent four hundred years carrying soil up mountains in bags for terraced gardens. Hence they came to be known as Firbolgs, which in Irish means bag carriers. Toughened by this toil they liberated themselves, went back to Ireland and wiped the floor with the Fomorians. They had barely settled down again when they were invaded by a strange race with magical powers called the Tuatha de Danaan. It was these people who are said to have given Ireland its name. One of their queens, a girl named Eri, was so beautiful that her fame spread throughout Europe, and Ireland came to be known as the Isle of Eri. In Irish, "Erin" would mean "of Eri." The Tuatha de Danaan also brought with them the Stone of Destiny, which was supposed to be the stone Jacob used for a pillow when he dreamed of the ladder to Heaven. Irish kings were crowned on it for hundreds of years, until one of them took it to Scotland. There it was stolen by the English and it now lies under the Coronation Chair in Westminster Abbey. You may have seen it on television.

Then, after three thousand years of Irish history, the Celts came to Ireland. They were known as the Milesians, or the Children of Mil, and they were supposed to have come by way of Spain. One day one of their princes, called Ith, caught sight of Ireland from the top of a high tower in the town of Briganza in Spain. You must bear in mind that it was a very clear day and a very high tower, and that the world was flat then. Curiously enough the Greek historian Herodotus, writing in the 5th Century B.C., also reported the Celts as being in Spain; and mysterious symbols found on a boulder at Clonfinlough in Central Ireland have been found to be identical with those in neolithic cave paintings in Spain.

Anyway, the story is that Prince Ith saw Ireland floating like a green cloud on the horizon and decided to take sail and have a closer look. He landed in Donegal, and found three sons of the King Dagda quarreling among themselves about their inheritance. He offered his services as a mediator and settled the dispute, but instead of leaving well alone he went on to reprove them for quarreling when they were fortunate enough to have such a beautiful country to live in. He was so eloquent in his praise of Ireland that the sons of Dagda came to suspect that he was going to return with an army and take it for himself, so they attacked his party. Prince Ith was killed, but a few survivors among his men brought his body back to Spain and told the King of the Milesians what had happened. He vowed to take vengeance for the death of Ith, and the country of the men who had killed him.

In that first confrontation between two types of Irishmen we see some national characteristics only too vividly displayed. Whether or not Ith and the sons of Dagda ever lived, their story would not have been told and retold for thousands of years if it had not been considered plausible, if the attitudes displayed by it had not been considered natural. A myth is a story honed down by the minds of a race like a piece of broken glass on the seashore, worn smooth until it tells more about where it has lived than about how it was created.

Ith is surely the prototype of the Celtic visionary, the man who can see beyond the horizon. He is the adventurer of the mind and the wanderer on the earth . . . and eventually the martyr, because he loses touch with reality. He voyages to a mystic land in the clouds, he interferes with the most generous of motives, he charms total strangers into harmony; but then, carried away by his own eloquence, he starts a worse fight than before and loses it. He typifies the generous idealism, the reckless extravagance of the Irish. But if he is the nation's superego, the sons of Dagda are the id. They are the primeval peasant, the kulak, the gombeen man, resistant to change and suspicious of novelty, but losing what they are trying to keep through quarreling among themselves. They and Ith have only one thing in common, and that is a love of Ireland, but on the one side too abstract and on the other too concrete. As Wilde was to put it two thousand years later, with considerably more relevance to Ireland than to the English he was addressing, each man kills the thing he loves. The history of Ireland can be seen as the struggles of men who love it in their different ways and lose everything. Through the generations the spiritual descendants of the prince have striven for an ideal Ireland glimpsed in a dream, and the latter-day sons of Dagda have fought tenaciously for their land. The princes die glorious martyrs and their names live forever; the peasants lose their land and are forgotten, as are the names of the sons of Dagda.

The avenging Milesian fleet had thirty ships with thirty warriors in each, but their main weapon was magic, their flashing invincible "swords of light." They are also described as tall and golden-haired, "like bluebells their eyes, like the sheen of a dark blue blade their eyebrows." With these clues the stories of the children join hands with the estimates of the archaeologists, because these are the racial characteristics of the Celts; and the swords of light must have been their iron weapons, which would indeed have been invincible to people armed only with bronze. And it is known that the Iron Age came to Ireland at about the same time that the Celts were being pushed westwards by the same invasion from Asia which was bringing down the Roman Empire.

The Firbolgs fought bravely, but eventually had to make peace with the invaders. Thereafter the two races lived together more or less peaceably, intermingling and producing the complexities of the Irish character. The Firbolgs left a legacy of many millions of small dark Irishmen and Irishwomen and some impressive fortifications, but little trace of their culture. A few strangely beautiful gold ornaments survive and a few carved inscriptions, but their language has been lost forever. No doubt some of it was absorbed into Gaelic, but there is no purer branch of the Celtic language with which Irish can be compared. The only clue to it is hidden in the rivers of Ireland. Most Irish rivers have descriptive names, like Blackwater, but there are some whose names mean nothing in Irish and these must have been christened by the Firbolgs. As the archaeologist Macalister put it, "The names of rivers are the oldest monuments of human thought."

As for the fearsome Fomorians, historians think that these existed too, in a special kind of way. There is archaeological evidence of a Neolithic invasion about 2000 B.C., and no doubt there was a battle then. But there are always two accounts of any battle, one from each set of survivors, and in the conversion of these stories into myth the contradictions are resolved in a very simple way. One battle becomes two, and both accounts become history. It is surely significant that in myth the Fomorians are in turn invaders and invaded, and that their opponents are also of the same people each time. The hated and hideous Fomorians are simply Them, seen from the point of view of the invaders in one account and from the point of view of the invaded in the other.

It would, I suppose, be going a little too far to surmise that the myth of the drowned Cesair and her companions is a folk memory of some hunters caught by the incoming tide on that land bridge from Scotland, but otherwise the myth-carrying children and the spade-carrying archaeologists seem to agree quite well. With one strange exception: the Tuatha de Danaan. What happened to those strange people with the magical powers, who gave Ireland its name and its Stone of Destiny, and ruled it for two hundred years? The archaeologists can give no answer, and the historians are equally baffled. Lady Ferguson in 1899 wrote of the Milesian invasion: "It is from these successful adventurers that most of our native families claim to trace their descent. But it is singular that while these Milesian representatives abound, and families with Firbolg ancestors are not unknown, no race, clan or family existing at the present time are reputed to have Tuatha de Danaan blood in their veins."

So we must go back to the children's stories for an answer to the mystery of the sudden disappearance from the scene of the Tuatha de Danaan. The children's explanation is, as you might expect, simple and straightforward, and it accounts for everything. Rather than accept their defeat by the Milesians the proud Tuatha de Danaan went underground, to a magically excavated system of souterrains marked by what are now known as fairy mounds, and there they live to this day. They have become smaller through the ages, but they retain their magical powers and use them to help or plague human Irishmen, according, presumably, to whether they reckon them to be Firbolg or Milesian. They are, simply, an unusually stubborn underground resistance movement.

So if you should happen to have an Irish name, and yet be not tall and golden-haired with black eyebrows, do not feel bad about not being a pure-bred Celt. You have powerful friends in low places.

5. Dragons, etc. in Ireland, Incidence of

They say that Queen Victoria used to sit down whenever she felt like it, without bothering to look around for a seat: she knew someone would always pop a chair under her in time. I used to think this confidence was impossibly smug, until one day I realized I had it to some extent myself.

That was while I was visiting a friend in Kansas City, the first time I was in America. We went into his back yard after breakfast and I made to sit on the grass. He warned me not to, on account of the chiggers. I had never heard of chiggers before, and as he explained their little ways to me I was filled with a sense of outrage. What sort of place was this, I thought, where a man could not even sit on the surface of his own planet? It was like being told that mothers' milk was unsafe for babies. And then I realized with some surprise that there must be in fact very few places in the world outside Ireland where you can sit down thoughtlessly on the grass without risking anything worse than a damp bottom.

It is well known that there are no snakes in Ireland. Neither are there any termites, poison ivy, mosquitos, chiggers or any other noxious creatures I still haven't heard of. For further reassurance perhaps I might refer you to Giraldus Cambrensis, secretary to Prince John, who visited Ireland in 1187 and reported:

. . . There are neither snakes nor adders, toads nor frogs, tortoises nor scorpions, nor dragons. It produces, however, spiders, leeches and lizards; but they are quite harmless. . . . It does appear very wonderful that, when anything venomous is brought here from other lands, it never could exist in Ireland. For we read in the ancient books of the saints of that country, that sometimes, for the sake of experiment, serpents have been shipped over in brazen vessels, but were found lifeless and dead as soon as the middle of the Irish Sea was crossed. Poison also similarly conveyed was found to lose its venom, disinfected by a purer air.

You can understand the difficulties this must involve for the Irish pharmaceutical industry. But on the other hand, as the Venerable Bede pointed out, "Almost all things in the island are good against poison. Indeed it has come to our knowledge that when certain persons had been bitten by serpents, the scrapings of the leaves of books brought out of Ireland were put into water and given them to drink, which immediately expelled the spreading poison and cured the swelling." And it was well known that if your garden was infested with noxious creatures, you had only to send for a few handfuls of Irish earth and sprinkle it thinly over the surface, whereupon all reptiles would depart with breathtaking speed, presumably into your neighbor's garden.

This property of Ireland was also useful in determining international disputes. For instance it was found that snakes thrived on the Isle of Man, conclusive proof that it belonged to Britain, not Ireland.

The situation in regard to frogs however has changed

since those days, and on this subject Cambrensis seemed eerily clairvoyant:

> *Nevertheless a frog was found, within my time, in the grassy meadows near Waterford, and brought to court alive before the Warden there and many others. And when the Irish had beheld it with great astonishment, at last Duvenold, King of Ossory, beating his head and having deep grief in his heart, spoke thus: "This reptile is the bearer of doleful news to Ireland." And he further said that it portended without doubt the coming of the English, and the subjugation of his own nation.*

True enough, ever since then Ireland has suffered from no shortage of either Englishmen or frogs.

Ireland is also deficient in earthquakes, tornadoes and volcanoes. The only volcanic eruption recorded in recent times was in 1788, when a newspaper correspondent reported that Knocklayde Mountain in North Antrim had become active again and a torrent of molten lava had engulfed the village of Ballyowen, immolating both the parish priest and the Presbyterian minister. This account was widely believed by many who did not know Knocklayde to be a gentle grassy mound, the most unlikely candidate for such dramatics you could imagine, and was quoted in books for the next fifty years. It was, of course, a piece of what is locally known as codology, by someone who had been following the fierce controversy then raging between two groups of geologists over some peculiar rocks discovered at Portrush nearby. The Biblical school of geologists had been fiercely denying the possibility of any volcanic activity having produced them, since the Flood would have put all volcanoes out of action.

As for hurricanes, the nearest thing there has been was the Big Wind of 1839, when herrings were found six miles inland. American hurricanes are usually subdued to westerly gales by the time they reach Ireland, though indeed they can still be quite severe. On the west coast of Ireland the thatch on the cottages is held down by ropes from which big stones are suspended. There are little summer whirlwinds, but they do no damage. Sometimes however they are accompanied by mysterious sounds, especially in the neighborhood of Lough Neagh. The geologist Praeger describes them as strange booming noises. But then Lough Neagh, the largest fresh-water lake in the British Isles, has always been a mysterious place. Many people say that near Aghalee and Ballinderry on a summer's day you can often hear the sound of children laughing, but there is never anyone there. In the 19th Century, before the motor car and the depopulation of rural Ireland changed the habits of the people, Lough Neagh was thronged with pleasure boats and picnic parties. Then the main roads bypassed it, and it was left to the wild birds and the fishermen and the happy ghosts of children. It still has, according to local tradition, the submerged city mentioned in the song "Let Erin Remember," the power of turning things to stone, and its own fresh-water mermaids called *Boheenas*. It certainly has it own species of fish, the pollan, though its main commercial product is the eel, despised in Ireland but appreciated in London as the Cockney delicacy of jellied eels.

That little summer whirlwind is known in the country as "a progress of fairies," and indeed fairies, "the lordly ones who dwell in the hollow hills," have for many country people in the past represented a greater peril than any mere phenomenon of nature. A farmer's wife is, for instance, in grave danger if she throws out dirty water after dark, for she may throw it onto a passing fairy, or worse still down a fairy chimney. Of course a good housewife would have her washing done well before dark, and generally it is remarkable that the requirements of the fairies are those normally observed by a conscientious wife and mother. Special domestic fairies called *cluricauns* punish the slovenly by turning the milk sour or putting the fire out or hiding things, but they reward the good housewife by giving her magical help, so that nothing gets lost and her house is always bright and clean. This strange state of affairs exists in other countries, I am sure, but the reason for it is not as well understood as it is in Ireland.

The most dangerous thing you can ever do is to disturb a fairy thorn. Country people will of course deny any belief in fairies nowadays, but often you have only to look over their shoulder to see a lone hawthorn tree in the middle of a field which has been carefully ploughed around for generations. If you are so tactless as to press the subject you will be told it would be more trouble than it is worth to remove the tree, but you will also probably be given an account of someone who tried, with invariably dire results. Some of these stories are very well authenticated. For example, at Lecale near Downpatrick a thorn tree was to be uprooted from the site of a new building. The workmen refused to touch it and the site superintendent had to tow it out himself; on the way a horse shied, causing an accident as a result of which the superintendent had to have a leg amputated.

A modern archaeologist writing on this subject in his new university building in Ireland comments wryly that from his window he can see a fairy thorn right in the middle of the science laboratories. When one reflects that the instinct of the average modern building contractor is to remove every tree within a beagle's howl of him, to quote a local unit of measurement, it is obvious that some extremely strong counter influence must have been at work. Some archaeologists surmise that this respect for the hawthorn is a survival of the pre-Christian religion of Ireland, as is the role of the mistletoe at Christmas. Certain trees were held sacred by the Druids, and were probably planted on graves. It may be that the sacredness of the fairy thorn is a subconscious respect for the dead, dimly surviving in the racial memory. If this is so it is indeed unlucky to disturb a fairy thorn, because a man who believes that what he is doing is wrong is very accident prone.

On the other hand, fairies are known to be repelled by iron, which gives support to the theory that they were the previous rulers of Ireland, defeated by the iron swords of the Celts. The horseshoe hung above the cottage door is a protection against bad fairies and, contrary to later superstition, it is not important whether it be hung upside down or not. The important thing is that it is iron. Similarly, women in childbirth must keep a knife by the bedside to prevent evil fairies from stealing the baby and substituting a changeling, though it must come in handy too for severing the umbilical cord. Fairies steal only boy children, and until recently it was quite common in the west of Ireland for little boys to be dressed in petticoats to deceive the fairies: a ruse which one fears might not always be effective in the modern world. If you are confronted by any supernatural being, it is sufficient just to say "cold iron," and you will be safe from harm. I call that a very useful piece of information; you may not appreciate it now, but you may remember it with comfort the next time you are in a lonely place at midnight.

Generally speaking, however, the relationships between the Irish and the fairies have been cordial. It is well known that fairies use eggshells for boats, so conscientious children have always driven a spoon through the bottom of their boiled egg to prevent the fairies from leaving Ireland. Nevertheless there is grave reason to believe that this strategem has not been successful, or that a considerable number of children have fallen down on the job, since it is believed in some parts that the fairies left Ireland the day after the Night of the Big Wind. On the other hand, some people in Ulster believe they were still there until 1852. In that year one of them gave an interview to a farmer in Ballinascreen and told him there was to be a great battle that night with the fairies of Connaught: if his side lost the people would know it because such and such a stream would run red; if the other side lost another stream would run red. But next morning all the streams ran red and the fairies were never seen again.

However, the supernatural population of Ireland remains large and varied and generally of a more congenial character than that of, say, Transylvania. The people of Kilkenny were once reputed to be werewolves, but have reformed. Even the pooka, a fierce phantom horse or huge black dog, is not reputed to do anything more malevolent than breathe on all the blackberries on November Eve, making them inedible. Admittedly the banshee heralds a death in the family, but the apparition itself is usually only of a woman wailing and washing bloodstained clothes, and in itself no more gruesome than many television commercials for soap powder.

Most noble families have a banshee, and it beats hell out of a Rolls-Bentley as a status symbol. The family of Doneraile in County Cork has not only the regulation banshee and several orthodox ancestral apparitions, but also a pooka in the form of a shaggy black colt, two huge phantom mastiffs, a spectral coach drawn by four headless horses, and a pack of ghostly huntsmen and ghostly hounds pursuing a ghostly stag. I must say that to me this smacks of vulgar ostentation.

In more restrained taste is the apparition of the Earl of Kildare, which once every eleven years rises from his grave in the Curragh and gallops on an enchanted horse shod with silver to the room of his Countess in the castle. When the silver horseshoes are quite worn through the Earl will return to life and rule all Ireland, and I think the respective governments should know when last seen the horseshoes were only the thickness of a sixpenny piece.

Among the less conventional apparitions are the Nine Green Cats of Ballydineen, who march continually up and down the glen between there and Byblox, crying "Ohee. Ahyeh!" I don't know why they do this. They may be worried by the Flying Yellow Dog, which is said to patrol the air space above Doneraile Bridge, but all he does by all accounts is wait for an equally mysterious Black Ram. When *he* turns up they both go into

Oldchurch Graveyard, and what they do there no one has yet ventured to ascertain.

In a special category of extinct animal ghosts is the Gray Cow of Goibnu, which used to appear regularly before Irish homes, offering a plentiful supply of free milk. Unfortunately one greedy housewife kept some for sale, and in disgust the Gray Cow plunged into the sea and was never seen again; unless of course it is the power behind the Free Milk Scheme in the English Welfare State.

On a more ethereal plane is the egg-shaped blob of yellow light which is to be seen in the vicinity of Bally-andrew, moving at walking pace about three feet above the ground. On closer inspection it turns out to be carried by a semi-transparent skeleton. But probably the most typical of all Irish ghosts is the Radiant Boy of the Mallow Road. This engaging young fellow, dressed entirely in dark blue and covered with bright stars, sits on a gatepost and makes continually as if to throw some sort of radiant missile at passersby, but never actually does it.

Far more perilous is the Hungry Grass. Anyone walking on a patch of this is attacked by a sudden overpowering hunger and will die unless he eats something at once. Another insidious danger is the Stray Sod: to walk on this is to lose one's way home. It is as if these ancient beliefs were a foreboding of a future in which all Ireland was to be covered with the Hungry Grass, and many people were never to see their homes again.

6. The Land of Saints and Scholars

In Bavaria in the 8th Century an Irish scholar called Fergil was denounced to the Pope for teaching the heretical doctrine that there were men living in another world under another sun. Fergil explained that all he had said was that the world was round and there might be people living in the Antipodes, a concept current in Irish colleges. The Pope was tolerant of these quaint fancies and indeed later made Fergil Bishop of Salzburg, thereby simultaneously denying him the immortality later conferred on Copernicus.

This half-forgotten episode is typical of how until comparatively recently the originality of Celtic thought has been underestimated. In many ways the ancient Celts were so far in advance of their time that they were ignored by their contemporaries, and forgotten by history. It has of course for some time been recognized that they preserved European culture in a period of barbarism, so that it has been said that during the Dark Ages the history of civilization was the history of Ireland, but the analogy many people have in mind is of a culture which is popped into the refrigerator to keep overnight. In fact the Golden Age of Celtic Ireland lasted a thousand years, and its function was more like that of a conservatory. The tender plants of learning not only thrived in the climate of Celtic civilization, but grew and evolved until they put forth flowers which had never been seen before, and spread seeds which took root in the barren soil of barbaric Europe.

The changes the invading Celts immediately made in the structure of Irish society were to affect the national character at its very roots. They introduced a new law of property and inheritance, by which the land of a father was held in trust for the family, to be shared equally among his sons on his death. This replaced the law of primogeniture which prevailed in other primitive societies, under which everything went to the firstborn. This system was to produce generations of young men who were proud, individualistic, independent, conscious of the equality and brotherhood of Man . . . and desperately poor. This Law of Gavelkind, as it was called, hindered the economic development of farming and was to lead eventually to the country's virtual destruction, but as the French historian Michelet observed:

> As this law of precious equality has been the ruin of the Celtic races, let it be their glory also, and secure to them at least the pity and respect of the nations to whom they so early showed so fine an ideal.

.The Celts applied their theories of equality even to the succession to the throne, which did not go automatically to the first-born as in normal monarchies. Under the Law of Tanistry it went to the "oldest and most worthy man of the same blood," which in the closely knit society of those times offered quite a wide field of choice. In practice the system bore an uncanny resemblance to the presidential system of democracy in the United States, in that kings were elected from among a number of candidates vying for public favor. The Celts even introduced a system of national conventions: every three years all the leaders and bards and law-givers gathered for six days of feasting and talk at Tara, where no doubt intrigue went on in peat-smoke filled rooms.

The authority of the king was presidential in character too. He could not change the law by himself or interfere with its operation, and in fact his executive power was limited to action in time of crisis and to external relations. If the state of the country deteriorated during his reign he was deposed and another king elected. Any blemish in his personal appearance made a candidate ineligible, a custom which seems to have returned with television.

This system of government produced, not surprisingly, a great number and variety of kings (the average reign was not much more than eight years) and a great deal of picturesque and violent history. This was the time of Deirdre of the Sorrows, of the tragic lovers Dermod and Grania, of the Great Cuchulain, of the Knights of the Red Branch and of the Fianna, and of countless other heroes and heroines who haunt every hill and valley in Ireland and live in the thoughts of every well brought up Irish child. It was this society which laid the foundations of Irish literature by creating and preserving what Funk & Wagnall's *Standard Dictionary of Folklore, Mythology and Legend* flatly declares to be "the finest body of folklore in the world."

It might be worth quoting the vows of the Fianna Knights to show what the Celts expected of the Nation's Finest:

*Never to seek a dowry with a wife, but to choose
her for her good manners and virtue.*
Never to offer violence to a woman.
*Never to refuse to any mortal in need anything one
possesses.*
Never to flee from less than ten adversaries.

Apart from knights like these, who coped mainly with
enemies of the state, and were really a sort of FBI, the
Celts had no system of law enforcement other than the
pressure of public opinion. The law itself stemmed from
custom and tradition and was preserved and interpreted
by a special class of bards called the Brehon. Essentially
it required that any man who did another man an injury
had to pay him compensation, and this included the
cost of nursing and maintaining him and his family while
he was unable to work. Anyone who defaulted on his
payments lost face in the community and was debarred
from receiving compensation himself. The same duty
lay on a man to look after his old or sick relatives
and the same penalties applied if he failed to do so. Everyone had the right to expect hospitality according to his
needs, and a duty to provide it according to his means.
The status of a man in the community depended not
so much on his wealth, but on the number of obligations
he voluntarily undertook towards his fellow men.

If a man persisted in ignoring his obligations the ultimate remedy was to fast against him. The aggrieved
person would sit outside his door and starve, to arouse
public opinion against the culprit. This ceremonial fast-
ing was such a standard legal procedure in Ireland that
in an early Gaelic religious poem there is an account of
Adam going on hunger strike against God to protest being

expelled from the Garden of Eden. The remedy was employed with rather more success in 1920, when Terence McSwiney the Mayor of Cork, starved himself to death in protest against the English occupation of Ireland, and nine of his fellow citizens set a world record with a hunger strike of ninety-four days. The English left the following year, public opinion in some quarters having reached the ethical standards expected in pre-Christian Ireland.

The Celtic system of welfare without bureaucracy and law without police can of course work only in a small community in which the difference in living standards between rich and poor is not excessive; but it is not to be dismissed on that account. One could argue that our modern system does not work at all, and indeed that a sense of civic responsibility cannot be preserved in large administrative units. Many people today, especially the young, seem to be inclining to the view that the solution to our problems lies in reverting to community units small enough to give everyone a sense of participation in decisions and responsibility for his own actions.

Such was the civilization which, halfway through its existence, encountered Christianity. According to legend King Conor in A.D. 74 died with rage on hearing of the Crucifixion, but in fact the Gospel was introduced to Ireland by St. Palladius, in A.D. 431. He had some limited success in Kerry, and ever since Kerry men have boasted that they were Christians before the rest of Ireland; the rest of Ireland usually replies that Kerry men had to be converted twice, and even then it didn't take properly.

Meanwhile, up North, a boy called Patrick had been herding sheep on a mountain near Ballymena. He was not an Irishman, having been captured during an expedition by King Niall to either Britain or France. When he grew up he escaped, made his way back home and began to study for the priesthood. But he had a vision in which a letter was delivered to him headed *Voice of the Irish*, in which they pleaded to him to return, and in A.D. 432 he landed in Ireland to convert the country to Christianity, the first mail-order missionary.

What happened then is recorded in some detail. Patrick made straight for the citadel of Tara and arrived at the Hill of Slane, ten miles away, on the evening of Easter Saturday. This was the day of the year on which it was his duty to light the paschal fire. But it was also a pagan festival to celebrate the beginning of summer, this being symbolized by the extinguishing of all fires throughout the country; a ceremonial fire was then lit by the Druids, from which all the other fires were re-ignited. It was a crime punishable by death to allow any fire until this was done, as Patrick well knew.

Preparations for the Druid ceremony were in full swing when a light was seen on the distant Hill of Slane, rapidly becoming a great glow in the darkening sky. The Druids ran to the king in anger, crying with a strange foreboding, "If that fire be not put out, it will burn forever."

The king and his Druids, in eight chariots, sped to Slane, where a great crowd of people had already gathered. Patrick came through them to meet the king, singing: "Some in chariots and some on horse, but we in the name of the Lord." The words were from the Bible, but the tune was his. The king was impressed by Patrick's courage, the people were charmed by the song, the Druids conceded defeat and the Church had entered into its estate in Ireland.

Or so the story goes. In fact the conversion of Ireland was by no means as sudden and complete as that account implies. The kings of Ireland remained pagan for another two hundred years, and even as late as 1844 votive offerings of flowers were placed by country people on the altar at Mount Collan in County Clare to the pagan sun-god Lug. In the previous century animals were still being sacrificed there.

It is true that the conversion was remarkably peaceful, which says a great deal not only for the tolerance of Celtic civilization but for the personality of St. Patrick. The only recorded casualty of his mission was King Aengus of Munster, who during his baptism had his foot accidentally impaled by the spike on the end of St. Patrick's pastoral staff without anyone noticing it . . . except, of course, King Aengus. The unfortunate monarch assumed it was part of the ceremony and stood uncomplaining, transfixed with holiness, through the remainder of the ritual.

There was of course in the Celtic civilization a great respect for learning and for freedom of expression, and Patrick started off with that advantage. But for its part the Church accommodated itself with considerable tact to the customs of the country, accepting its laws and social system and indeed reinforcing them. To the average peasant in his day-to-day life the transition from his pagan ways to those of the true faith cannot have been very marked. The paschal fire must have looked very much the same as the one the Druids used to light about the same time of the year. The Celtic New Year, November first, became the Feast of All Hallows, but the pagan ceremonies continued on the day before, as indeed they still do. So did those for the winter solstice, with the sacred mistletoe and holly. The worship of Brigit, the pagan goddess of fire and wisdom, was transferred to St. Brigit, and so on. So successful was this assimilation that in the 12th Century an Irish poet could address the Almighty as "O Salmon of Knowledge," a clear allusion to the magic salmon of Irish myth which swims in the Boyne and, having fed on the nuts from the Tree of Knowledge, contains all wisdom. The god Finn owed his gift of second sight to having touched this salmon with his thumb, and thenceforth needed only to bite his thumb to arrive at the solution to any problem—a device still followed by humans with varying success.

The early Irish Church, on its own, also arrived at some doctrines which seem so sensible that one regrets that the Roman Branch did not see fit to accept them. It should for instance be more generally appreciated throughout Christendom nowadays that while the rest of the world is undergoing the horrors preceding Doomsday, Ireland will not only be spared that anguish but will have a friend at court. Exactly one week before it will have been covered by a soft green flood, while the inhabitants are being judged by St. Patrick.

It is well known that St. Patrick introduced the shamrock as a symbol of Ireland by using it as a visual aid to explain the mystery of the Trinity (which accounts for the fact that many Irish children think of God as small, green and vaguely triangular), but unfortunately the fact seems to have been so well known that nobody bothered to write it down until about 150 years ago. Indeed the first mention in literature of the shamrock in connection with Ireland was in the 16th Century, when English writers reported it to be part of the Irish diet. I realize this is disturbing news, like the French finding a frog's leg foisted on them as a national symbol, or like the Americans discovering that their eagle is really a turkey, but I'm afraid there is worse to come. Not only is the shamrock not peculiar to Ireland, but the Irish themselves are not sure which plant it is. They think they know, but not so long ago an interfering naturalist carried out a sort of shamrock census. One March he wrote to people all over Ireland asking for specimens of the True Shamrock that Grows in Our Isle, and then planted them and waited for them to flower. The obnoxious busybody then claimed to identify no less than four different varieties of trefoil, none of them unique to Ireland. In fact the word shamrock in Irish simply means "little clover." And, to pile horror on horror like Pelleas on Melisande, I read some years ago that the home crop had failed and supplies were being imported from Czechoslovakia. Oh well, I suppose it doesn't do to worry too much about trefoils.

In any event retribution was not long delayed, because shortly afterwards the Irish lost a case they had taken against a German firm for using the shamrock as a trademark. I am still waiting for fate to overtake the Japanese, who produce great quantities of fake Irish souvenirs. Admittedly they mark them with a statement of origin, but since there are two official languages in the Republic of Ireland all they have to do is stamp them "Made in Japan" in Gaelic, and very pretty it looks too.

Even the status of St. Patrick himself is not free from doubt. The members of the Episcopalian Protestant Church of Ireland point out that St. Patrick's mission to Ireland was inspired by an angelic visitation and not by the Church of Rome. (The official emissary was of course St. Palladius and it is true that St. Patrick was severely criticized by the Church authorities of his day.) St. Patrick's own statement, "I declare myself to be a bishop," is adduced as further evidence that he was acting on his own. Since both his ecclesiastical authority and his spiritual mission came directly from God, the Episcopalian Protestants conclude that the Church of Ireland is a true Apostolic and Catholic Church, owing no allegiance to the outfit in Rome. Or, in effect, that St. Patrick was a Protestant. It is an interesting theory, if not one I would care to advance too loudly in an Irish-American bar, especially since in view of the doubt as to St. Patrick's place of birth there is the dreadful possibility that he was an English Protestant.

Whatever the truth of it, it is a fact that the cathedral which St. Patrick founded is a Protestant one (in the crypt can still be seen the outlines of his little wattle church) and so is the one where he died and where he is said to be buried. Nevertheless the North of Ireland, where all of these are and where the Church of Ireland has its greatest strength, is less enthusiastic about the Saint. The Government takes St. Patrick's Day off, but it is not a public holiday. A few years ago the situation was even more anomalous, in that the pubs in the South were closed on St. Patrick's Day, and many people came north to celebrate. In those days the only place you could get a drink in Dublin on March 17th was at the Royal Dublin Society's annual Dog Show, and the number of dog lovers in the city was remarkable.

After St. Patrick the most notable early Irish saint was St. Brendan, who has a mountain named after him in Kerry. It has one unusual feature, as I found when I climbed it a few years ago. On the seaward side are long lines of large white stones, obviously arranged by some human agency. I was sure I had discovered some rare archaeological curiosity, until I eventually realized they spelled out EIRE, and had presumably been placed there by a thoughtful government for the benefit of confused transatlantic pilots. You have no idea how strange it feels to be living in a labeled country, like a cartoon character. At least they didn't spell "Made in Japan," and if one knows more about St. Brendan it is curiously appropriate that the sign should be on his mountain.

St. Brendan had an oratory on the summit of the mountain, and he had a view not only over all the mountains of Killarney but over the vast horizons of the Atlantic. There, in what Coleridge called "the green light which lingers in the west," one can sometimes see the faint outlines of another land. This, the Irish believed, was the enchanted island of Hy Brasil, the Isle of the Blessed, the Land of the Ever Young. It was visible to mortals every seventh year, but if once touched by a human fire, even by the flight of a kindled arrow, it would become subject to the ordinary laws of existence and remain in the real world as a paradise for men. The last reported sighting was in 1872, by T. J. Westropp, the same one that counted all the ruins in County Clare. His account is in Volume XXX of the *Proceedings of the Royal Irish Academy*:

I myself have seen the illusion three times in my boyhood, and even made a rough coloured sketch of it after the last event, in the summer of 1872. It was a clear evening, with a fine golden sunset, when, just as the sun went down, a dark island suddenly

appeared far out to sea, but not on the horizon. It
had two hills, one wooded; between these, from a
low plain, rose towers and curls of smoke. My mother,
brother and several friends saw it at the same time.

St. Brendan set out to find Hy Brasil, in a coracle
of hide stretched over an osier frame such as is still used
by the fishermen in the West of Ireland. The Atlantic
had no unknown terrors for him, since Irish missionaries
had already sailed as far as Iceland in these frail but seaworthy craft. After many weeks' sailing St. Brendan came
to a region of mist and cold, and what appear unmis-
takably from their description to have been icebergs and
walruses. Turning south he made his way into a region
of warm clear water, with translucent seaweeds and
colored fish, and islands covered with palm trees. He
sailed through this for eight days and came to a great
land, now thought by many to be Florida, in the region
of the Everglades. It was a paradise of flowers, gaily
plumaged birds with melodious song, food growing from
the trees and perpetual sunshine. The contemporary
Irish account anticipated the publications of the Florida
Chamber of Commerce.

> *There may not rage of frost, nor snow, nor rain*
> *Injure the smallest and most delicate flower;*
> *Nor fall of hail wound the fair healthful plain.*
> *That noble land is all with blossoms flowered,*
> *Shed by the summer breeze as they pass;*
> *Less leaves than blossoms on the trees are show-*
> *ered,*
> *And flowers grow thicker in the fields than grass.*

St. Brendan continued inland for five weeks, until he came to a great river. There an angel appeared to him and told him that this country was reserved for another time and for other teachers than he, and he should return to Ireland. But that he should tell what he had seen.

This St. Brendan did, to such effect that the account of his travels was the mediaeval equivalent of a best-seller for hundreds of years and was eventually to inspire Columbus and give encouragement to those who sponsored him. If you choose to believe implicitly in the legend of Hy Brasil, and who is to say that you shouldn't, then St. Brendan not only discovered America but brought it into existence with the first camp fire he lit on it. But if you disbelieve both it and St. Brendan, there is still no denying the fact that he had some part in the discovery of America, in 1492 if not eight hundred years earlier.

However, there is more to St. Brendan's claim than the inherent plausibility of his account. Professor Sauer of Berkeley cites evidence of Irish occupation found by the Norse settlers, who knew America as "Great Ireland," and certain ceremonies of the Algonquin Indians traceable to Gaelic Christianity. After deep study he has concluded that the Irish geographers of the 9th Century were working from reality in their accounts of St. Brendan's voyages. And Leif Erikson, who lived in Massachusetts long before Columbus was born, spoke of legends of an "Irish man of God and of the sea." It has even been suggested that the reason Cortes was so well received by the Aztecs was that he was thought to be a compatriot of St. Brendan's.

The legend of Hy Brasil, or Tir na n'Og, the Land of

the Young, was so tenacious that it continued to appear
on maps until the 17th Century, and indeed in 1721
the Portuguese Government sent an official expedition
to locate it. The name was finally bestowed on Brazil
in South America. The only Tir na n'Og I know of in
the modern world is in the Mount Stewart demesne in
County Down, where it is the name given to a lonely
walled garden on the far side of the lake from the house.
In this quiet place there rest the members of the family
who will never grow any older.

Brandenburg in Germany is also named after St.
Brendan, one trace among many of the first great dispersal of the Irish which was then taking place. Irish
missionaries were founding monasteries and universities
in Iceland, Scotland, England (Oxford), France, Switzer-
land, Germany and Italy. They penetrated into Africa
and into Russia as far as Kiev.

The learning of these scholars was founded largely
on that of Greece and Rome, because that of the Celts
was not yet written down. The pre-Christian Celts were
almost certainly familiar with both Greek and Roman
writing, but were always reluctant to use it. This was
partly because their learned classes had a vested interest in their memories, having spent up to twenty
years training for their professions. To acquire a Doctor-
ate as Poet-Chronicler, for instance, a candidate had to be
word perfect in at least 350 long narratives, together
with the genealogies and topographical distribution of
the principal families, the etymology of names and the
events of Irish and foreign history. In addition he had
to have such complete mastery of the intricate artistic
and technical disciplines of the seven kinds of poetry
which were his craft that he could extemporize a poem

on any subject at a moment's notice. The Celts were very conscious of the dangers of distortion during transmission, and the complex rhyme and rhythmic construction of Celtic poetry must have developed largely as a sort of running check on accuracy.

To be fair to the Celtic professional classes, however, their reluctance to entrust their learning to writing was more than a reactionary resistance to automation. In a turbulent society their method of preserving knowledge was simply more efficient than any that could exist until the invention of printing. A book cannot flee from destruction nor fight for its life. So the tradition of oral learning continued, even after the clergy had been absorbed into Celtic society. The monks wrote assiduously in their monasteries, but mostly devoted themselves to copying the Scriptures and other documents associated with the doctrines and philosophy of their Church. Little note was taken of native Celtic culture except for the Brehon Laws, the system of personal responsibility and public opinion, which had been absorbed into the Church's teaching following the report of a mixed commission chaired by St. Patrick himself. It is for this reason that we have today several large volumes of Brehon Law, but only stray traces of information about the equally massive body of Celtic thought in other fields. It was not until the twilight of Celtic culture, nearly a thousand years after St. Patrick, that a few monks in the comparative security of their monasteries wrote down all that remains to us of the civilization which was breaking up around them.

The only ancient Celtic writing which has survived consists of a few stone inscriptions in the strange Ogham script. This was an alphabet comprised entirely of short straight lines developed for sending short messages by notches cut in a stick, a sort of telegraphese, but it was equally suitable for carving inscriptions in stone. After the advent of Christianity stone inscriptions were of course in Roman lettering, and Ogham completely disappeared. Or at least so it was thought until the remarkable case of Rex v. Collins, reported by Praeger in *The Way That I Went*. In the 19th Century a farmer called Collins, who lived near the Old Head of Kinsale, was prosecuted by the local police for not having his name and address on the side of his wagon. A local antiquary was able to get him off by proving that the name and address was written on the side of the cart, in Ogham. It was fortunate for Mr. Collins that the archaeologists had recently succeeded, after much high-powered thought and learned research, in deciphering the Ogham stone inscriptions; but he must have wondered why they didn't just ask people like him in the first place.

Although the Irish churchmen spreading through Europe were not familiar with all the intricacies of ancient Celtic thought, they had after all been brought up as children in that civilization and took some of it with them to Europe. When writing in Latin, for example, they tended to be influenced by the poetry of their own country and are now widely credited with introducing the rhyme into European verse. The Irish were then, as now, passionately devoted to music and their performers had reached a standard of proficiency which astonished visitors. Music historians now believe it was they who introduced harmony and polyphony into European music, which until then had known only plain chant. As for art, the German historian Ludwig Bieler came in 1963 to the conclusion that:

Irish art . . . is not only unique in the Middle Ages, it is also the first, and in the West the only, example of an abstract art in an articulate civilization which was still spiritually integrated. . . . One of the determining factors that shaped Carolingian art, its spirit can still be felt in the romanesque art of the 11th and 12th Centuries. Gothic art broke away from this path and took a new direction. We at present stand at the end of the way which the art of Europe has since taken. Our eyes are opened again for the appreciation of Irish art, which is one of the glories of our Western heritage.

There was at this time an Albanian quarter in the city of Armagh. I came across this remarkable statement in an old book and was about to pass it on to you when I realized that the author was thinking of people from Alba, the Latin name for Scotland, and that in honesty I must deprive you of the picture of the quiet little town of Armagh swarming with swarthy Balkans. Nevertheless, it is not all that far from the truth. People did come from all over Europe to study in Ireland, and even to the sons of kings it was a place to marvel at. Prince Alfrid of Northumbria wrote:

> *I travelled its fruitful provinces round*
> *And in every one I found*
> *Alike in church and palace hall*
> *Abundant apparel and food for all.*
> *I found God's people rich in pity*
> *Found many a feast and many a city.*
> *Piety, learning, fond affection,*
> *Holy welcome, and kind protection.*

Poets well skilled in music and pleasure
Prosperous doings, mirth and pleasure.
Flourishing pastures, valour, health
Long-living worthies, commerce, wealth.
Sweet fruits, good laws for all and each,
Great chess players, men of truthful speech.
Candour, joyfulness, bravery, purity,
Ireland's bulwark and security.

In the troubled renascence of its civilization Europe forgot its debt to Ireland, as a child forgets what it owes to its mother. It wasn't until the 17th Century that it began to think back, and the Englishman William Camden wrote: "Our Anglo-Saxons of that day used to flock together to Ireland, as a market for learning; whence it is that we continually find in our writers concerning holy men of old, 'he was sent away to be educated in Ireland.' . . . It would appear that it was from that country our ancestors received the first instruction in forming letters, as it is plain they used the same characters which are still used in Ireland. . . . Ireland which is now for the most part wild, half savage, and destitute of education, at that time abounded in men of holiness, piety and splendid geniuses, while the cultivation of literature elsewhere in the Christian world lay neglected and half buried."

Here perhaps is the second fascination of Ireland. Just as a child never really forgets its mother, it may be that we who are the products of that civilization which it nurtured, subconsciously recognize our affinity with the land which still has some of the all-embracing warmth and welcome which Prince Alfrid described. But what happened to our mother? How did her people of "splendid geniuses" become in a few hundred years "wild, half savage and destitute of education?"

7. The Most Distressful Country

It's the most distressful country
That ever yet was seen,
For they're killing men and women
For the wearing of the green.

Some blame Ireland's doom on a woman and some blame it on the Church, alternatives eerily similar to those offered for the downfall of her hopes in the time of Parnell. The woman in question was called Dervorgilla, the red-headed wife of a prince of Connaught, but old enough to know better. She took off with Dermot, the King of Leinster, and her husband came after her with an army. Dermot invited the English to help him, and they outstayed their welcome. In a play of Yeats he has these two accursed adulterers wandering desolately down the ages pleading to the people of Ireland for forgiveness. But "Oh, never, never, shall Dermot and Dervorgilla be forgiven."

Then again, some people say the English might have gone home again if they had not felt they had a right to be in Ireland. This right was given to them by Pope

Hadrian IV, who awarded Ireland to Henry II of England in the airy way popes had in those days of disposing of territories which did not belong to them. In the same way one of them gave North America to the King of France and South America to the King of Spain, another of those generous gestures like selling the Brooklyn Bridge which involve a lot of trouble to everyone except the donor. Curiously enough Hadrian IV was an Englishman, and unfortunately there has never subsequently been an Irish pope to give Ireland back to the Irish.

The motives of Hadrian IV were to keep friendly with England and to bring the excessively independent Irish Church into proper submission to Rome, and the papal bull showed a firm grasp on these and other practical realities.

Since then you have signified to us, dear son in Christ, that you desire to enter into the land of Ireland, in order to subdue the people to the obedience of laws, and extirpate the vices which have taken root, and that you are also willing to pay an annual pension to St. Peter of one penny for every house therein, and to preserve the rights of the Church in that land inviolate and entire, we . . . are well pleased . . . that you should enter that island. . . . It is likewise our desire that the people of that country should receive you with honor and venerate you as their master: provided always that the ecclesiastical rights therein remain inviolate and entire, and reserving to St. Peter and the most holy Roman Church the annual pension of a penny from every house. . . .

One might say that an annual rental of about ten thousand dollars a year was not as good value as, say, the Louisiana Purchase; but that is to overlook the fact that the price was to be levied from the Irish. In other words, they were not only to have their country taken from them, but were required to pay for the privilege. Nevertheless the papal grant was loyally accepted by many generations of Irish Catholics and indeed it was not until some 150 years later that its validity was even questioned.

But while it is tempting to be able to blame some one person for all the sufferings of Ireland, I should think that both Dervorgilla and Hadrian might well be forgiven. The real villain of the piece was geography. Nothing could have saved Ireland but to be towed a thousand miles further into the Atlantic. As long as she was only a few hours' sailing from England, and easily accessible from France and Spain, she was for England a back door that must be safeguarded at all costs.

It would have helped if she had even been a different shape. A desperate schoolboy once in an examination, trying to make his molehill of knowledge look like a mountain, described the country as "an island with water round the edges and land in the middle." This description would have been more illuminating if it had read "an island with land around the edges and water in the middle." Geographers usually describe Ireland as saucer shaped, and while one would hesitate to dine at their homes if this is the sort of crockery they use, it is true that most of the mountains are around the coast; the interior is a flat plain full of bogs, lakes and rivers.

This makes for impressive mountains and a picturesque coastline, but it is also a text-book example of guerilla country. In history it has meant that Irish unity has always been precarious, and could not be preserved at all while the plains were occupied by hostile forces; and that the hostile forces have always been exposed to raids from the mountain fastnesses. The English could not simply defeat the Irish Army and make a treaty. The whole country had to be "pacified," using the standard anti-guerilla techniques of savage reprisal and indiscriminate massacre, and effectively occupied.

It was this problem which was to defeat the English for seven hundred years, as it had already defeated the Norsemen. For two hundred years Viking raiders had plundered Ireland, destroying priceless books and stealing exquisite objects of art which ever since have been turning up in Scandinavian tombs, with no resistance from the monks or the gentle Christian communities which surrounded their monasteries. A folk memory of this helplessness persisted in the custom common in Ulster until a few years ago of withholding the right arm of a male baby from baptism, to preserve its pagan strength. Eventually Brian Boru (the first member of the Kennedy family to make his name in history) unified the Irish and beat the Norsemen in battle, in 1014 at Clontarf, but even before then Ireland had won in the sense that most of the settled Norse communities had already been integrated with Irish life. In the absence of fresh reinforcements from abroad the Norse in Ireland disappeared quietly into history, leaving only castles and memories and a great many tall blond Irish.

This almost magical power of Ireland to make any stranger Irish in two generations is attributed by many to the climate. The unpredictable vagaries of the weather incessantly inculcate, it is said, alternate moods of optimism and pessimism, of grandiose imaginings followed by a sense of the futility of all human endeavor. Like the poster for a village garden fete, where a list of gay attractions is followed by the ominous words, "If wet, in the Scout Hall." The bewildering variety of the scenery is rivaled in the skies. The prevalence of a westerly airstream over the island, broken by the great mountains of the coast, fills the sky with perpetually changing clouds, often moving at different speeds and giving the impression that the land itself is moving. Mountains are always in sight, and change according to the weather from brooding masses disappearing into the clouds to the shimmering blue boundaries of other worlds. In misty weather their summits float in the sky like islands, and even on the clearest day the moist air softens the light, so that the land is like one seen in a dream. It is no accident that Irish writers have always been fascinated by the difference between appearance and reality.

Whatever the reason for the spell of Ireland, it was a phenomenon that surprised and frightened the English, who like things to be as they appear, and to stay that way. Nothing, it seemed, could be trusted in Ireland, not even themselves. The problem of remote and rebellious Connaught, for example, seemed to have been solved when it was subdued and entrusted to the stern and reliable Anglo-Norman family of De Burgos in the early 14th Century. But almost immediately, historically speaking, the solid De Burgos had disappeared and in their place were an Irish family called Burke, speaking Irish, wearing Irish clothes, following Irish laws and defying English authority. This sort of thing happened so rapidly that the Irish were absorbing English settlers faster than the English could send them.

On at least one occasion the Address to the Parliament in Ireland, which was supposed to represent the English occupation, had to be translated into Irish before the members could understand it.

The phenomenon continued despite drastic laws against the use of the Irish language, clothes and customs, and it worried the English to distraction. Indeed one could almost regard the Anglo-Irish conflict as a war of self-defense by the English, in protection of their way of life. Certainly a great deal of the fighting in those days was between the "Old English," who had become Irish, and the "New English," who had not yet succumbed, with the native Irish caught in the middle.

The English English would no doubt have accepted the situation with their usual practicality, if it had not been for the fact that there was a vital ideological element in the struggle: another respect in which it curiously resembles the situation in Vietnam. Under the feudal system of English society, a nobleman held his land at the pleasure of the king, who theoretically owned everything, and the nobleman in turn could dispose of his serfs as he thought fit. This system made for efficient farming, and the English saw nothing wrong with it for Ireland, which then as now they regarded as a pleasant but inefficiently run sort of place full of impractical people who could do with a spot of discipline. But the Irish regarded themselves as all free men, owned by no one, and the land as belonging to the people. They still followed the Celtic Law of Gavelkind, under which a man's land was not his to do with as he liked, but was held in trust to be divided equally among his sons. The result of this conflict of laws was that an English king would gracefully bestow a great estate in

Ireland on a loyal subject; the grateful recipient would retire to Ireland, swearing undying loyalty on behalf of his descendants; and then, it seemed, the moment the king turned his back the land was divided up among a crowd of fiercely independent foreigners owning allegiance to no one. Obviously the land would be lost to the Crown forever unless something was done about it, so the whole process was started over again.

"Ireland would be easy to govern," said a British prime minister once, "were not its people intractable and all its problems insoluble." One is inclined to wonder why they bothered trying, until one appreciates that the longer the problems lasted the greater was the incentive to try to solve them. The richer England became, the more powerful her enemies, and the less she could dare to have a hostile base across the Irish Sea. Moreover she was now a Protestant country, and Ireland was still Catholic, like her enemies. England felt she was fighting for her way of life, for her very existence, even for God.

These were powerful motives, and by the beginning of the 19th Century they had produced effective results. The last vestiges of Celtic civilization had been obliterated, Irish commerce and industry had been suppressed, and the land of Ireland was firmly in English hands. None of these three results would have been possible without the other two. The destruction of Irish culture was accomplished by a system of laws described by Dr. Johnson as worse than the persecution of the early Christians and by Edmund Burke as a machine of perverted ingenuity for the degradation of a people and the debasement of human nature itself. Their degradation and impoverishment meant that there was no native Irish community in which an English settler could mix and become absorbed, any more than he would mix with his farm animals.

An added safeguard was provided by the fact that most of the English aristocrats who owned the land now lived in England, and conducted their affairs through agents whose only instructions were to get as much money as they could. This the agents accomplished with great efficiency by the simple expedient of auctioning tenancies. This produced a sort of competition in impoverishment, for the highest bidder was the man willing to accept the lowest standard of life for his family. If he made any improvements to the land the rent was promptly raised, and if he couldn't pay he was evicted, so the people idled their lives away in hopelessness. The system so impoverished both the land and the people that in 1839 it was said that the Irish farmer had a lower standard of living than the poorest serfs in Tsarist Russia. He lived in a mud hut with a bundle of furze for a door, and no window but a hole in the roof to let the smoke out. A horrified French visitor said, "I have seen the Indian in his forest and the Negro in his chains and I thought then I had beheld the lowest term in human misery, but I did not know the lot of Ireland." And yet, compared to what was in store for the Irish, this was happiness and prosperity.

The system was made possible by the potato, introduced from America. It so thrived in Ireland that for three weeks' work in the year a tiny plot of land could keep a whole family. Since there was no hope of advancement for a man, there was no reason for him to delay getting married: when his sons grew up they would live as he did, and keep him in his old age. So land was divided and subdivided and subdivided again. By 1841 the population had grown from two million to eight million, all competing with one another for land and all dependent on the potato, a foodstuff which does not keep and cannot be stored. In 1845 the crop was attacked by the potato blight, and in 1846 it was wiped out. The entire food supply for millions of people became in the space of one week a mass of rotting vegetation. A million men, women and children died from starvation and typhus. By 1847 three million survivors were being fed from soup kitchens, but it was too late; the Irish were leaving Ireland. In the years of the Famine itself over a million left, and by the turn of the century four million had gone. In one generation, by death and emigration, the population of Ireland had halved. By 1880, two-thirds of all the people born in Ireland were living outside the country.

One might wonder how people so poor could afford to travel to America, even in the "coffin ships" of those early days, and it was a question that puzzled people at the time. The answer that eventually emerged was that the Irish were mounting their own rescue operation.

The fantastic scale of this operation was first noticed when the United States Postmaster General reported that the number of letters to the United Kingdom had risen from two million a year to six million a year. Further inquiries revealed that over five million dollars a year were being sent by people in the United States to people in Ireland, and a further uncountable number of people in America were buying steamship tickets and mailing them over. The Irish in America were throwing a lifeline through the mails. It seemed that every Irish man and girl who survived the trip was working till he dropped and sending home his wages to bring over brother or sister or sweetheart, and that in this way entire families were being ferried across the Atlantic, one by one. By 1884 the amount of money alone arriving from America had risen to eleven million dollars a year, and this at a time when a good wage was a dollar a day.

Much of this money had of course to be used to pay the rent and buy food, and it kept many thousands of people alive in Ireland. "The American Letter" became part of Irish folklore. A ritual grew around its reading and the term itself became synonymous with good fortune and well-being. A man passing another in the street and asked how he was would say, "Fine, like the American Letter." Even today in Ireland, when you get a lucky break at golf or tennis, your partner will describe it as "money from America."

Historically, there was more significance to this money from America than immediate good fortune. For thousands of years Ireland had been the last outpost of European civilization, but now its place had been taken by America. The Land of the Ever Young that the Irish had seen long ago in a dream was now a reality, accepting the wretched refuse of Ireland's teeming shore and giving them new life. As Ireland had once saved Europe, America was now coming to the aid of Ireland.

The more serious minded immigrant Irish saw quite clearly that the money they were sending home was ending up in the pockets of the landlords and preserving the system which had caused the Famine. From the armies returning from the surrender at Appomattox came cries of "Dublin next." The Irish in the States contributed half a million dollars to finance armed invasions of Canada and Ireland. They failed ignobly, but the English were alarmed. Their Home Secretary wrote:

> In former Irish rebellions the Irish were in Ireland. ... Now there is an Irish nation in the United States, equally hostile, with plenty of money, absolutely beyond our reach.

He was right to fear Irish-American money, for in three years it financed Parnell's Land League to the tune of over a million dollars. Parnell himself addressed a joint session of Congress and twelve hundred branches of the League were formed in America. In three years it became the most powerful movement in Ireland, and Parnell the greatest Irish leader since Brian Boru.

The objectives of the League were to end by nonviolent means the iniquitous system of annual tenancies at "rack rents." Heretofore the Irish farmers had tried to deal with the problem by the simple expedient of forming secret societies to kill any landlord or agent who evicted a farmer from his land, and any other farmer who took it over. But many of the landlords were in England, the agents were well protected, and the competition for land so intense that many Irish farmers were willing to risk death to feed their families.

Parnell showed a better way. "Shun him on the roadside when you meet him; shun him in the shop; shun him in the fair green and in the market place and even in the place of worship . . . as if he were the leper of old." This weapon, first used against a landowner in Mayo called Boycott, proved dramatically effective. Not only was it deadly in itself in a community as intimate as that of Ireland, it was a weapon a child could use. Without breaking the law the whole people could show their solidarity. Thus encouraged they broke into open war against the landlords. It began with rent strikes and organized armed resistance against evictions, and developed into full-scale guerilla warfare as armed bands called "Moonlighters" roamed the country at night beating up or murdering agents and informers and destroying the property of landlords.

Within two years the British Government passed an Irish Land Act providing for a form of rent control. It brought an immediate reduction in rents amounting to twenty million dollars a year, a good return on the Irish-American investment, but it was more important as the first in a series of land acts which within a generation were to transform Ireland from a country of landless peasants to a nation of independent farmers. Without Irish-American money and support all this would hardly have been possible. The Irish in America had secured for their brothers the land of Ireland, which they themselves would never see again.

More important still, they had given them back their pride and strength. The people who had been groveling in degradation now stood tall enough to see the end of their seven hundred years of suffering.

8. Mayor Lynch and Captain Boycott

To illustrate the peaceful state of Ireland in the reign of Brian Boru, it was said that a young girl could walk naked the whole length of Ireland carrying a gold ring on the tip of a wand, without being molested in any way. I don't know if this experiment was actually tried, but it would certainly be a more interesting way of assessing the delinquency rate than compiling criminal statistics.

Less dramatic but possibly equally significant was the episode described by Helen O'Clery in the *Pegasus Book of Ireland*. She reports an apparently authentic case of a girl who came to work in Dublin and mailed most of her wages home every Saturday. At least she thought she did, but the new mail boxes in Dublin were rather like the litter bins, and each letter was actually thrown into the garbage. Nevertheless each one arrived at its destination a little grubby but intact.

There were no people under heaven, said the Attorney General of England under James I, who loved equal and impartial justice better than the Irish. In the thousand years that elapsed between the adventures of those two young ladies, that love of justice was to be tested in various sadder and more violent ways.

While Columbus was discovering America, the mayor of Galway was paying a civic visit to Cadiz. At that time

Galway had a brisk trade with Spain and Italy, and indeed a few months previously Columbus had called there to replenish his supplies and recharge his spiritual batteries by attending mass in Galway Cathedral, only a few dozen miles from where St. Brendan had left on the voyage which had been his inspiration. The mayor of Galway was so hospitably received by a Cadiz merchant called Gomez that he invited his host's son for a holiday in Ireland. The young Gomez had much in common with the mayor's own son and the two became fast friends. Unfortunately their common interests came to include the same local girl. In a fit of jealousy which will be readily understandable to anyone who has ever fallen in love with a Galway girl, the mayor's son killed the young Spaniard and threw his body into the sea. Then, overcome with remorse, he confessed and gave himself up. The judge was his father, who sentenced him to death.

But the son was well loved by the people of Galway, and nobody could be found to carry out the sentence. Indeed an angry mob tried to release him from custody. The mayor dragged his son from their hands and bolted the door. Then, in full view of the crowd, he hanged his own son in his own bedroom.

The name of this man who put Justice before Love was James Lynch, and it is one of the ironies of history that his name should be given not to the sort of deed he did, or even the one he tried to prevent, but to a more evil one than either. However the most significant thing from our point of view was the behavior of the Irish mob. When they saw what Lynch had done, and that there was no help for it, they simply withdrew and left Lynch alone. The door he had bolted behind him was opened neither by them nor by Lynch himself, who ended his blighted life behind it in perpetual silence. Outside, his deed came to be regarded by the Irish with the awed admiration they accord to virtues which they do not themselves possess. Their respect for the law has always been accompanied by a determination that it should not be allowed to interfere with justice, and by justice they mean not an abstract principle but what they feel to be right.

Once they went to war by way of appeal against a judicial decision—that in the case of Finnian v. Columba, circa A.D. 600. St. Finnian had a book he was so jealous of that he refused to lend it to St. Columba, so St. Columba borrowed it without permission and furtively copied it. St. Finnian caught him at it and demanded both the book and the copy. St. Columba refused to surrender his own work and the dispute was referred to King Dermid. He ruled "To every cow her calf: so to every book its copy," a ruling which laid the foundation for the modern law of copyright, which prevents your copying out all this book in longhand and selling it for fifty-nine cents. The judgment was however hotly resented by St. Columba, who retreated into the wilds of Donegal muttering darkly that Dermid was little better than a crypto-pagan. It didn't take much to start a fight in those days and the king of Connaught argued Columba's case with an army in the notorious Battle of the Books. Over three thousand men were killed and Columba was overcome with remorse. He went to his confessor, who decided he must suffer the ultimate penalty of those days, exile from Ireland.

The book which caused all this trouble still exists, an heirloom of the O'Donnell family of Westport, County

Mayo. They entrusted it to the McGroarty family, and many of these hereditary custodians gave their lives to protect it in the succeeding centuries. In the 18th Century an O'Donnell took it to Europe and died there, and the book was lost for a while. In 1802 it was recovered by Sir Neal O'Donnell, and in 1814 the sealed brass and silver casket which contained it was opened by Sir William Betham, the Ulster King at Arms. He was promptly sued by Sir Neal O'Donnell's widow for doing so without her permission but everyone was so curious that no one blamed him. Inside the casket was a small wooden box, very much decayed, and inside that a copy of a Psalter written in a "neat but hurried hand."

There must, of course, have been other causes for the Battle of the Books, but nevertheless it is a fact that good law was held in very high esteem in those days. The ability to hand down a good legal judgment was rated the most important attribute of a king, and indeed the greatest of all Irish kings, Cormac McArt, owed his throne to this. His father's throne had been usurped by one Mac Con and Cormac himself was leading incognito the life of a shepherd in Tara, employed by a poor widow. The widow's sheep strayed onto the royal lawn and the false king ruled they should be forfeited for the trespass. "No," demurred Cormac, "the sheep have eaten only the fleece of the land, and in justice only their fleece should be forfeited." The wisdom of this judgment was acclaimed by everyone, even Mac Con, who unguardedly cried, "It is the judgment of a king," and thereby effectively relinquished his throne.

Of course where there is no police force, no effective law can exist unless it is whole-heartedly accepted by public opinion: and conversely, public opinion can enforce its will without laws, a fact which was forcefully brought to the attention of Captain Charles Cunningham Boycott, agent for the estates of the Earl of Erne in County Mayo. One morning he awoke to the fact that he did not exist. His servants had left, shops would not serve him, tradesmen did not call, the blacksmith was even unable to see his horse, the postman did not deliver his mail . . . though some say he made an exception for bills. More serious still, no one came to harvest his crops despite every inducement. In desperation he arranged with the British government for the importation of fifty laborers and an escort of two thousand soldiers. The miniature army disembarked from special trains at the station fifteen miles away, in pouring rain. Strangely enough there did not seem to be any local transport available of any sort whatever, and all the shops and pubs were suddenly sold out. Hungry and tired, the laborers and their massive bodyguard trudged the fifteen miles through the downpour to Captain Boycott's place and proceeded to eat him out of house and home. Eventually the crops were harvested, and then Boycott found no one would buy them.

He came to no permanent harm, however, and indeed lived to a ripe old age. They say he was delighted to find his name appearing in dictionaries, and I am sure he would be pleased to know it is now a word even in Russian.

The idea of boycotting is supposed to have been suggested to Parnell by an American journalist called James Redpath, but it was simply a re-emergence of the old Celtic system of law enforcement noted by Julius Caesar. He observed with interest that among the Celts a person who failed to comply with a judicial decision was "excluded from sacrifices and deprived of honor and normal society," and that this sanction seemed remarkably effective. Since from the Irish point of view there was no justice in English law, they created their own law and enforced it, unwittingly following the example of their ancestors.

They had some reason to be dissatisfied with English law as it was administered in Ireland. The English government assumed they had a right to rule in Ireland and came to believe they had a duty to do so since the Irish were incapable of self-government. It followed that anyone who attacked English rule or the rights of property with which it was associated was not just a criminal but a treacherous and seditious ingrate . . . a description which at times must have seemed to fit the entire population of Ireland. But however impeccable this reasoning and however altruistic its inspiration, its results in practice were often difficult for the Irish to distinguish from tyranny.

Such difficulty must surely have been felt by a certain respectable Dublin brewer called Hevey during the strange series of events that befell him between 1798 and 1802. They began when he wandered idly into a courtroom where a man was being tried for some offense against the state, and found to his surprise that he knew the prosecution witness. He was a rascal whom Hevey had sacked. Hevey got up and told the court the man was not to be trusted, and was so convincing that the prisoner was acquitted.

A day or so later Hevey was accosted in the street by the Crown prosecutor, a Major Sirr, and told he would be taught to meddle. As a first lesson, Hevey was seized and thrown into prison. After seven weeks he was sent for by the warden, a Major Sandys, who told him he had noticed he had a fine horse. He had better make it over to Major Sandys because he would certainly be hanged and he could not travel to the other world on horseback. Hevey gave an order for delivery of his horse, if only because the document would let his family know he was still alive.

Next day he was taken to Kilkenny for court martial. A proclamation was issued offering a pardon and a reward to anyone who would give evidence against him. The lure was accepted by a wretch lying under sentence of death, and on his evidence Hevey was convicted of treason and himself sentenced to be hanged.

However, before the execution the papers came by accident to the notice of Lord Cornwallis, the representative of the King of Ireland. Disgusted, he ordered Hevey's release, though he had not at that time power to reform the machinery of state which had imperiled him. Back in Dublin the intrepid Hevey went to Major Sandys at the prison and asked for his horse back. "Ungrateful villain," said the indignant major, "is this the gratitude you show to His Majesty and me for our clemency?" Unabashed, Hevey took an action for the return of the horse. The major climbed down, fearing no doubt for all the other such acquisitions which would flow out through the floodgates which a successful action by Hevey might open.

With his life and his horse and his position in society restored, Hevey must have thought his troubles were over. But three years later he met Major Sirr, the prosecutor, again in a coffee house. Sirr said Hevey should have been hanged. Hevey said Sirr was a slanderous scoundrel. Sirr had Hevey seized and thrown into prison again.

Next day Sandys appeared on the scene again and told Hevey he was being imprisoned for his insolence to Major Sirr, and would not be released until he signed a submission. Hevey refused, and issued a writ of habeas corpus. Sirr and Sandys countered with a forged warrant on a charge of treason. At length the suffering of his family and the ruin of his business brought Hevey to sign the submission, but on his release he took an action against Sirr for assault, battery and false imprisonment. He was represented by the great Irish advocate John Philpot Curran.

Curran's address to the jury was even more moving than the circumstances would appear to us to require. His difficulty was that it was the practice in those days for the government to pack, suborn and intimidate juries in Ireland until they could be relied on to produce verdicts satisfactory to the Crown. An opposing attorney had not only to convince the jury of the justice of his client's case, but to persuade them that they should risk their lives or livelihood on his behalf and that this sacrifice on their part would be worth while.

Curran began by saying that he did not intend to address himself to their "proud feelings of liberty." The time for that was past. "Where freedom is no more, it is a mischievous profanation to use her language." He therefore did not call for "a haughty verdict, that might humble the insolence of oppression, or assert the fancied rights of independence." All he asked was some reparation for his client's extreme suffering.

Having reassured the jury that they were not expected to be heroes, Curran went on to recount in detail the history of Hevey's ordeals, with much savage irony at the expense of Sirr and Sandys. Sandys was in court and Curran defied him to deny a single syllable, an invitation which was not accepted.

No country governed by settled laws or treated with common humanity, Curran said, could furnish any occurrences of such atrocity. But it is the destiny of Ireland to be the scene of such horrors, "and be stung by such reptiles to madness and to death." No printer in England, he pointed out, would dare to publicize any of the thousand atrocities like the present one; except in the report of a law case. If the jury found for Hevey, England would know something of what was being done in Ireland in her name.

It was not that he hoped this could make any general impression on the morality of the country whose property we are become. A nation had no heart. What had Spain felt for the murders and robberies in America? Nothing. "Her bosom burning with all the fury of rapine and tyranny; her mouth full of the pious praises of the living God and her hands red with the blood of his innocent creatures, she yet prided herself as much as England ever did on the elevation of her sentiment and the refinement of her morality."

Practical justice and humanity, Curran pointed out, were virtues that required laborious acts and mortifying privations. He was not so foolish as to expect them. But there were other feelings in England which could be appealed to with more prospect of success. "A stupid preference and admiration for self, an affectation of humanity, and a fondness for unmerited praise: these you may find, for they cost nothing." When outrages of this kind were held up to the world as sample acts of

English authority, England must become odious to mankind unless she let fall some reprobation on those immediately responsible. If she were not ashamed to employ instruments like Sirr, at least she could see that it could not be in her interests to "encourage such an infernal spirit of subaltern barbarity, that reduces man to a condition lower than that of the beast of the field."

Curran stressed again that "England knows nothing of our situation. When torture was the daily and ordinary system of the executive government, it was denied in London with a profligacy of effrontery equal to the barbarity with which it was exhibited in Dublin." It did not serve any purpose to tell England about the situation in general terms. "When you endeavour to convey an idea of a great number of barbarians practising a great variety of cruelties upon an incalculable multitude of sufferers, nothing defined or specific finds its way to the heart, nor is any sentiment excited, save that of a general, erratic, unappropriated commiseration. . . . The real state of a country is more forcibly impressed on the attention of another by a verdict on a subject such as this, than it could be by any general description. . . . If any man shall hear of this day's transaction, he will well know that outrages like this are never solitary. . . . I am therefore anxious that our masters should have one authenticated example of the treatment which our unhappy country suffers under the sanction of their authority; it will put a strong question to their humanity, if they have any; to their prudence, if their pride will let them listen to it; or at least to that anxiety for reputation, to that pretension to imaginary virtues of mildness and mercy, which even countries the most divested of them are so ready to assert their claim to."

Curran had thus convinced the jury that some good might come of their recognizing the justice of his client's claim and, to allay their apprehensions for their own safety, had contrived to imply that the authorities might actually conceivably be grateful to them for doing so. He was, he stressed again, not asking them to be indignant or contumacious towards the English, but merely moderately to suggest to them "that for their own sakes, and for their own interest, a line of moderation might be drawn; that there are excesses of infliction that human nature cannot bear." Carried away, the jury returned shortly with a verdict for Hevey of £150 damages, with costs.

One could wish that Hevey's story might end on that triumphal note, but happy endings were rare in Ireland in those times. In fact the persecution of Hevey continued, his business was ruined and his reason undermined, and he died shortly afterwards a lunatic and a pauper. The reptiles that English rule had brought to Ireland had indeed stung him "to madness and to death."

But no one would now say that Curran's efforts had been in vain. In retrospect he can be seen to have been addressing not just the twelve men in the jury box, but all the people of Ireland and England, and he did not lack an audience. Speeches like this, all the more remarkable for having been delivered from the briefest of notes, were taken down with care and published with admiration. In 1807 a collection of them went into three editions in four years. In 1843 another book of them was published. And in 1853, in a preface to yet another volume, Thomas Davis wrote:

Then might you have seen the crimson-clad judge

—and the packed jury—and the ferocious prosecutor—and the military gangs from the castle crush round the dock, wherein were the fearless and the true, and threaten with voice and gesture that little dark man who defended the prisoners. He scowled back upon their threats. "You may assassinate me," said he, when their bayonets were levelled at his breast, "but you shall not intimidate me!" They could better have hoped to drive the stars from heaven by their violence, than force John Curran by threats to surrender one hair of his client's head. . . .

He came inspired by love, mercy, justice and genius, and commissioned by heaven to walk on the waters with these patriots, and lend them his hand when they were sinking. He pleaded for some who, nevertheless, were slaughtered; but was his pleading in vain, therefore? Did he not convert many a shaken conscience, sustain many a frightened soul? Did he not keep the life of genius, if not of hope in the country? Surely, he did this all the time; and his speeches now and forever will remain less as models of eloquence than as examples of patriotism and undying exhortations to justice and liberty.

Nevertheless, if they had not been models of eloquence they would not have been undying. In the Hevey case more than in any other Curran seems to be addressing a third audience, posterity. Hevey was not one of the "patriots" to whom Davis refers, but a mere innocent bystander, an ordinary man caught up in the tides of history and preserved like the grain of sand in a pearl. Through Curran we feel something of what it must have been like to live in that Kafka-like world of irresponsible authority. The only remarkable thing about Hevey was his steadfast and touching faith, against all odds, that justice was obtainable through the law. For many years the obstinate courage of ordinary men like Hevey and the eloquence of courageous lawyers like Curran were to be the only defense of a helpless people.

Curran's daughter Sarah had been secretly engaged to Robert Emmett, leader of the abortive insurrection of 1803, and died heartbroken in Europe after his execution, "far from the land where her young hero sleeps." With Emmet's death armed resistance in Ireland virtually ceased for a century, but England's war with France continued and was largely responsible for the severity with which anything resembling sedition in Ireland was dealt with. For instance a schoolmaster called Wright was sentenced to five hundred lashes when a note written in French was found in his pocket, although there was good reason to believe it had merely been written by one of his pupils. The magistrate, the notorious Thomas Judkin Fitzgerald, himself dragged his victim by the hair to the flogging triangle in the square at Clonmel and supervised the punishment. After fifty lashes Wright's entrails were exposed and an army officer tried to stop the proceedings. Fitzgerald insisted on another hundred lashes and the body was thrown aside to die.

It has to be remembered that punishments like this were meted out by the English ruling classes to their own people, for example the British Army and Navy, of which the country was so proud; there it was stopped only on the insistence of Parnell, who had "the cat" exhibited in the British Parliament. But the atrocities against the English common people are forgotten because English history is the history of the ruling classes: the atrocities against the Irish are remembered by the Irish because their history is that of the people. And to the credit of English law as well as Irish advocates, some amend was made in the case of Wright. Nursed back to health by his fellow prisoners he made a miraculous recovery, sued Fitzgerald in the High Court and was awarded damages of five hundred pounds. Less creditably, the English government passed an Act of Indemnity to protect Fitzgerald and indeed he was made a baron. However, his ambition to found a noble line was not to be fulfilled. According to Rex Mackey's fascinating book *Windward of the Law,* his son came to a violent end, his grandson tied a stone around his neck and threw himself in the River Suir, and his great grandson accidentally strangled himself while showing his playmates how his forebear used to hang rebels.

Not even the High Court could be relied on for justice, as evidenced by the notorious case of Captain Frazer. This British soldier, drunk after dinner, accosted an old man called Dixon who was mending a cartwheel outside his cottage and charged him with disobeying the curfew. When Dixon pointed out that his cottage was outside the curfew area the gallant captain cut him to pieces with his sabre, inflicting no less than nineteen wounds. The coroner's jury returned a verdict of willful murder but the judge, to whose court Captain Frazer had been escorted in anticipated triumph by the regimental band, acquitted him on the following remarkable grounds: "Captain Frazer was a gallant officer who had only made a mistake. If Dixon was a good man, as he was represented to be, it was well for him to be out of this wicked world; but if he was as bad as many others in the neighbourhood it was well for the country to be quit of him."

Examples of arrogance such as this were becoming sufficiently rare to cause scandal. An effective alliance existed between the people of Ireland and the best elements of the legal profession, of both religions and races, to bring the practice of English law into closer accord with its pretensions. There was also a powerful third party in the coalition, the people of England. Throughout the 19th Century English juries, by steadfastly refusing to convict defendants when they knew the penalty would be excessive, forced revision of the savage penal code; and simultaneously the extension of democracy in England was weakening the repressive powers of the land-owning class. Appropriately enough, the last public execution in England, in May 1868, was of an Irish rebel who had blown up the wall of a prison to release a comrade.

The same processes operated and the same reforms applied in Ireland, with some local variations. Irish juries had not the same freedom of action as English ones, but made up for it by a more ingenious perversity. One jury returned a verdict of not guilty on a charge of rape on the grounds that the accused had "not used any more force than was reasonably necessary in the circumstances." A judge once despairingly released a prisoner "without any stain on your character save that of having been acquitted by a Limerick jury." Castlebar acquired a similar reputation, enshrined in verse by James Comyn, QC:

*Of all judicial utterances the bitterest by far
Is "the safest place in Ireland is the dock at Castlebar."*

The same judge who complained at Limerick once announced: "Some people think my jurisdiction is limited to cases not exceeding fifty pounds. It is not. I can give a decree for fifty pounds costs on the higher scale, enormous expenses and a load of abuse from the dirtiest tongue in Christendom." The practice of law in Ireland required an agile and unconventional mind, and the profession was acquiring a great number of more or less engaging eccentrics. One judge opened his court with, "It is time for Crown business. The crier will please search the public houses and bring in the magistrates." At Rathkeale the court was regularly attended by a harmless lunatic called Jones, who believed that he had no skull and had to keep his hat on to prevent his brains from catching cold. The court there habitually opened with a slightly amended form of the official proclamation: "Hear ye all manner of persons that this Court is now open and any desirous of transacting business herein come forward and you shall be heard and Mr. Jones may keep his hat on, God Save the King."

After Parnell the Irish Nationalist party acquired something of the influence of a shadow government, and the humanization of the law in Ireland accelerated. For the first time in a thousand years the law in Ireland began to approximate the mind of the people. In Maurice Healy's charming and nostalgic memoirs of those days, *Tales of the Munster Circuit,* there is a story which offers a heartwarming contrast to what was happening a hundred years previously.

In 1905, in Cork, relates Healy, a little barefoot post office messenger was charged with having got an underage girl into trouble. Some letters from him to her were read in court, and one phrase lived in Healy's memory all his life:

Far away from where I am now there is a little gap in the hills, and beyond it the sea: and 'tis there I do be looking the whole day long, for it's the nearest thing to yourself that I can see.

Healy watched the judge and saw a tear trickling down his nose. When the prosecutor had finished reading the letter the judge said, "Mr. Ronan, these two young people seem to be very fond of one another. Why couldn't they get married?"

The prosecutor said it cost money to get married. "I don't suppose it would cost a lot," said the judge. "Will the post office take him back if I bind him over?" It seemed they would, so the judge called up the girl. "Do you love the boy?" "I do, my Lord." "Will you marry him?" "I will if he'll ask me, my Lord." "Now, prisoner, do you hear that? Will you marry her?" "There's nothing I'm more wishful for, my Lord." "There now, that's settled; are the girl's people here?"

They were, and a little procession followed the judge into his room, where the bride was endowed out of his own pocket. And I hope, said Healy, that they lived happily ever afterwards. I tried to find out if they did, but the news editor of the Cork *Examiner* tells me the files were destroyed in the fire of Cork in 1921. They had a good chance anyway, because apart from the

Troubles in which that fire occurred, the worst of Ireland's sufferings were over.

The new nation which their child would have helped to build shows traces of its history in its attitude to law. Dishonesty and non-political violence is rare, but authority as such is still suspect. Government restrictions on individual liberty, such as liquor licensing laws, are regarded as bureaucratic window-dressing to be evaded by right-minded citizens, and public notices are consistently ignored out of a firm conviction that they do not apply to one's own circumstances.

Nevertheless the Irish continued to have an almost mystical respect for the concept of Law. One of the first acts of the revolutionaries of Sinn Fein was to set up their own courts of law in opposition to those of the British, and they soon acquired such a high reputation that they were even resorted to by their political opponents. The civil war which followed the treaty with England was largely fought on the niceties of the interpretation of the Oath of Allegiance to the British Crown, and even the desperate gunmen of the IRA always claimed to be acting perfectly legally. They did not steal property, but "requisitioned" it on behalf of what they claimed was the lawful government, and sometimes even paid compensation, with money "captured" from British banks. They did not murder or even assassinate their opponents, but executed them, a distinction which was rather lost on their victims. When captured they refused to plead, declaring the court to be an "illegal assembly." Sometimes this attitude was carried to almost alarming lengths. Behan tells a story of how in 1920 the IRA held up the manager of the Ford factory in Cork and told him they intended to "requisition" some of his lorries. The manager, a quick thinker and no stranger to Ireland, pointed out that his factory was United States property, and they could not under international law requisition the property of a neutral power. The IRA man was only momentarily dismayed. He scribbled on a piece of paper a Declaration of War on America by the Irish Republic and handed it over. "Now," he said, "the keys of them lorries."

The Irish also retain their readiness to resort to law and their disinclination to accept an unsatisfactory result. The most striking recent example was probably the case of the Irish writer Honor Tracy. She wrote for an English newspaper an article about a parish in Ireland where, it seemed, the people were being coerced by their parish priest into providing him with an expensive new house, though they themselves were living in poverty. It was the priest's practice, she claimed, to read out the names of subscribers in church in descending order of value, and his appeals for money were a great deal more audible than his sermons. A parish priest whom the cassock fitted sued the newspaper for libel and they prudently settled out of court, publishing an apology. However everyone had reckoned without the redoubtable Miss Tracy, who refused to accept this tidy solution. She promptly sued the newspaper herself on the grounds that its apology was a libel on her, won her case and was awarded several thousand dollars in damages—a development which must have made the unfortunate English newspaper resolve never to publish anything about Ireland again.

As this case implies, the vacuum created in Ireland by the removal of English repression has to some extent been filled by local institutions. It may be that today a young girl could walk naked the length of Ireland carrying a gold ring on the tip of a wand without being molested, but she would certainly be charged with indecent exposure.

9. The Wild Geese

If every Irishman in the world went home to Ireland, and with the weight of their numbers the little island sank beneath the waves, St. Patrick would not have to disturb their soft green grave on the Day of Judgment. Crowds of witnesses from other nations would come to give evidence on their behalf, carrying a strange collection of hastily gathered exhibits for the defense: South American stamps with the picture of a man called O'Higgins. Street signs wrested from the Avenue de Clery in Paris and O'Donnell Street in Madrid. The battle honors of British regiments and much of English literature. The American Constitution and the Declaration of Independence. A French cab and a Model T Ford with pneumatic tyres. Behind them a French truck with the Arc de Triomphe. And behind that again a long line of trailers filled with the libraries of the world and with historians still finding fresh evidence of what the Irish have contributed to the history of their countries.

There have been four great dispersals of the Irish. The scholars of the Dark Ages were the first, and they left books and schools and universities all over Europe. But since they wrote even their names in Latin, their gifts to European culture were virtually anonymous. No one even seems to know why a French cab should be named after the Irish Saint Fiacre, unless like Elijah he ascended to heaven in a flaming chariot.

Next came the merchants and craftsmen. English dominion in Ireland had shrunk to an area of some twenty miles around Dublin called The Pale (hence the expression, "beyond the pale") and Ireland had become prosperous again, while Englishmen in Ireland were begging their bread. Through their eighty-eight ports the Irish traded with France, Spain, Portugal, Italy, Germany and the Netherlands, importing wine, iron and spices and exporting linen, rugs, clothing, shoes, gloves, timber, marble, ropes, baskets, glass, furniture, hardware, pottery, whiskey, and food. Irish merchants settled all over Europe in numbers we can assess only from such clues as that as early as the 12th Century there was a hospital for the Irish in Genoa, and Irish craftsmen roamed Europe designing, building and beautifying churches, castles and great houses. Their services were so highly organized they were able to offer guarantees: "A master was appointed for each art, who was bound to indemnify the purchaser for any damage arising from the ignorance or fraud of the mechanic." The links with Europe were so close that when the English government wanted to communicate urgently with Spain they sent the messenger via Galway.

Such wealth aroused the jealousy and greed of English traders and their Tudor monarchs, who were very efficient in their own way. When they had finished, "the flourishing towns of Ireland sank into ruins and the people lay dead in thousands upon the fields." The second dispersal of the Irish ended with the obliteration of their trade and industry, leaving only the ruins of the great port installations of Limerick, Galway, Waterford and Ardglass, and the incalculable contribution of thousands of anonymous exiled craftsmen to the arts and industries of Europe.

Being good craftsmen themselves, the English would have liked to do a thorough job. "It were good with the sword to destroy all the inhabitants of that realm for their wickedness, and to inhabit the land with new." But lacking modern techniques for this sort of thing they reluctantly concluded that some "poor earth-tillers of the Irish" might be retained, "which be good inhabitants." For the rest, it was death or exile, and precautions were taken that the "earth-tillers" did not rise above themselves by acquiring property or education. For some hundreds of years thereafter young people with intelligence and enterprise had no choice but to leave Ireland. Families starved themselves to send their bright children to be educated in France, and there were so many of them that the French word for boy, *garçon*, became the Gaelic word *gossoon*. But few of them returned, for there was no employment for them in Ireland except as lawyers, who were desperately needed to unravel the legal complexities involved by the vicissitudes of English rule. Hence the courage and quality of the Irish legal profession. No one can estimate the gain to Europe of these generations of brain drain, or the irreparable loss to Ireland. Or indeed the loss to England caused by the hatred and distrust of her engendered by Irish exiles in every European capital, which lasts to this day. General De Gaulle has Irish blood. Among the more obvious examples are the first president of the French Third Republic, General Patrice de MacMahon; French aristocrats with such even more unlikely names as the Vicomte O'Neill de Tyrone; and above all, the Irish Brigade of the French Army. Louis XIV once complained they gave more trouble than the whole rest of his army, and was told that was what the enemy said.

It was the Irish Brigade which drew England's attention most forcibly to its loss. At Fontenoy the Irish won the battle for the French, charging furiously on the English with cries of "Remember Limerick," and George II said mournfully, "Cursed be the laws that deprive me of such subjects." Limerick was to be remembered because it was there that in 1691 Patrick Sarsfield and his men laid down their arms on a treaty that was later dishonored by the British, and there that he and his eleven thousand men left Ireland forever. These were the Wild Geese. In the next fifty years another half million Irishmen followed them, to fight the English on every battlefield in Europe, and half a million died. There is little left of that third great dispersal but names like Dillon, O'Moran, Kilmaine, Lally and Warren on the Arc de Triomphe, and a glory never to be forgotten by either Irish or English. Kipling saw their spirit in the Irish Guards in the First World War, and wrote:

Old days. The wild geese are flying
Head to the storm as they faced it before;
For where there are Irish there's memory undying
And when we forget, it is Ireland no more.

The Irish Brigade had fought the English in India, and even in England itself with Bonny Prince Charlie.

When the American War of Independence broke out, General Dillon pointed out to the French Government that for the hundred years of its existence the Irish Brigade had always claimed the privilege of being placed in the forefront of any battle against the English, and asked that he and his regiment be sent to fight in America. His request was granted. But many more Irishmen were already in America, having come by a strangely different route.

The Tudor policy of clearing Ireland of its people so as "to inhabit the land with new" had been carried out most effectively in Ulster, the province which had always given most trouble, and it was settled with solid reliable Scottish Protestants. But hardly had the English finished congratulating themselves on this solution when they found the loyal Scots had somehow turned into rebellious Ulstermen. Many of them were Irish by parentage as well as adoption, for Scotland had originally been colonized from Ireland. They lived on good terms with their dispossessed Catholic neighbors, those who had survived and crept back from hiding, and often helped them evade the laws which prohibited Catholics from owning land. A Catholic would have the land made over to a Protestant neighbor, whose family became the legal owners, on the unwritten understanding that the Catholic family could use it as theirs and have the title to it when the law made that possible. There were many instances of this, and none was ever recorded in which faith was broken. Thus did common sense and kindly feeling triumph over the foolish wickedness of politicians and preachers, as it does today.

England wrote off the Ulster Scots as Irish, and suppressed industries in Ulster as in the rest of Ireland. The

Ulstermen successfully resisted the diabolical system of annual tenancies at rack rents which was ruining the land and the people in the south, but the landlords did nearly as well for themselves by granting only short leases and auctioning them when they fell due for renewal. Indeed they added an extra refinement to this torture of their tenants by allowing nobody to bid twice. This meant of course that a man who wanted to make sure of keeping his home had to bid far more than it was worth. At a terrible cost in privation and worry this system made for efficient farming and a hard-working and thrifty people, but all their work and worry did not bring them prosperity. The vast sums they paid out in rent were spent in England and the country suffered from what would nowadays be called a balance of payments problem. In those days they knew it as famine. An English newspaper in 1729 described how the Ulster people "crowded along the roads, scarce able to walk, and infinite numbers starved in every ditch in rags, dirt and nakedness."

So began the fourth and greatest dispersal of the Irish, the one that is still going on. First the scholars had left, and then the merchants and craftsmen, and then the leaders and poets and soldiers: now it was the ordinary people.

Most of the Ulster people who went to America in that first wave did so as a considered decision, weighing up the perils against the promises of America. The promises were made in newspaper advertisements by shippers and land promoters, who also sent agents around the country touting for America, addressing crowds and leaving passage tickets in the local shops. The New World was sold over the counter with the groceries. The perils were known to them through Ulster's linen trade with America. They knew that the ships described in those glowing advertisements were really offering less than two square feet of deck space per passenger, between decks less than five feet apart, with no portholes. That many of them were unseaworthy and that there were lifeboats only for the crew, passengers being regarded as freight. That the voyage would last from eight weeks to three months, if they survived storms, calms, pirates, fever and starvation. And that in America they would have to work even harder than they had at home, and fight Indians as well.

On the other hand they would be free men, and own their own land, and they already had a pioneer tradition. So during the 18th Century over half a million Ulster people came to the New World, nearly half the entire present population of the province. By the American Revolution they and their descendants comprised about a third of the population of Pennsylvania and occupied more than half the seats in its assembly. They had also fanned out from New York (advertisements in the Belfast *Newsletter* advised passengers "in the street called Broadway, ask for Wm. Smith, Esq.") and from Charleston along the Shenandoah and other valleys parallel to the Blue Ridge Mountains, into Virginia and the Carolinas towards the unknown West.

In the American trouble with England the English settlers were divided in their loyalties, but the Ulstermen were wholeheartedly for independence. President McKinley said "they were the first to proclaim for freedom in these United States," and they made up more than half the troops of Congress. Washington said that if defeated everywhere else it was among these men he would make his last stand for liberty. Charles Thompson of Maghera, County Derry, wrote out the official copy of the Declaration of Independence, five Ulstermen signed it, including John Hancock, another Ulsterman printed it and another was secretary of the Congress that accepted it. An Ulsterman was chairman of the committee of five who drew up the Constitution. George Henry Knox and twenty-one other Revolutionary generals came from Ulster.

Theodore Roosevelt described these Ulster-Americans as "strong and simple, powerful for good and evil, swayed by gusts of stormy passion, the love of freedom rooted in their very heart's core. . . . They were of all men the best fitted to conquer the wilderness and hold it against all comers." Daniel Boone was one of them. Davy Crockett may have been born on a mountain top in Tennessee, but his father was born in Derry. No one can say how much these men, the embodiment of the pioneer virtues, contributed to the American character; but it is certain they contributed much to American history, including fifteen presidents. Three of them were the only first-generation immigrant presidents the country has ever had; Andrew Jackson commented that he only just qualified for the presidency, having been conceived in Ulster.

Dispersing as they did to build America in the wilderness, many of these Ulster families disappeared into the bloodstream of America. History has tended to overlook them, in favor of other ethnic minorities who preserved their separate identity, forgetting, for example, that the movement for the abolition of slavery began among the Ulster Protestants of South Carolina, Tennessee and Kentucky, forty years before it was heard of in

New England. (In 1820 John Rankin declared it was safer to make Abolition speeches there than in Boston.) But the essential contribution of Ulster to America was recognized well enough in England at the time. In the British Parliament Lord Mountjoy flatly declared, "We have lost America through the Irish."

Stonewall Jackson, Sam Houston, Horace Greeley, Edgar Allan Poe, Harold Ross, Robert Fulton, Stephen Foster, Samuel Morse, Charles Stewart. By a strange quirk of history the most obscure of these Ulster-Americans was to be the most significant. Charles Stewart was an admiral in the War of 1812, commanding the U.S. warship *Constitution*. But more important he had a beautiful daughter called Delia, and she fell in love with a visiting Englishman of the old political family of Parnell. The son of their marriage inherited the political skill of his father's family, the love of freedom of his mother's family, and all the determination of both. An alliance had been made in the New World to remedy the wrongs of the Old, through the descendants of both the peoples involved. By the time Charles Stewart Parnell had grown to manhood the third party in the alliance was forming itself in America. The Great Famine had started in Ireland and the Catholics were coming.

If the Ulster Protestant helped build the American Dream of the rural pioneers, the Catholic immigrant awakened their descendants to urban reality. With a few exceptions, like one John Ford who went to farm in Michigan and bred a grandson who took an interest in automobiles, virtually all the four million refugees from a dying Ireland settled in the cities where they landed. They had no money to travel any further, and what they earned they sent home. Anyhow, they had no other place to go. Cutting peat, grubbing potatoes and fighting bailiffs were no apprenticeship to work an American farm.

There was, however, one field in which they were experts without ever having entered it, one tool of which they were masters without ever having used it. To the acquisition and use of power the Irish Catholic immigrant brought all the frustrated expertise of a man who has starved on a desert island with an encyclopedia of cookery.

It had been only too obvious in Ireland that the machinery of government was a mere cloak for the nakedness of the landlord power structure. The law was perverted, justice a travesty, and democracy in the modern sense did not exist. Few people could vote and the ballot was not secret. To vote against the landlord's candidate meant eviction, and the landlords conveyed their majorities to the polls like cattle. In any case, political activity in the normal sense was impossible, since the English government had with generous impartiality made illegal any organization in Ireland "appointed by delegation or having any representative character."

In such a society the ways of survival were devious, dangerous or dishonest. The ban on political agitation was countered by inventing the modern political party, in the form of Daniel O'Connell's Catholic Association, membership open to anyone who could pay a penny a month. The dues were collected by the clergy, who thus took the place of a party structure. With the funds so acquired and the incontrovertible evidence of mass support they supplied, O'Connell was able to win the right for the Irish to send Catholic Members of Parliament to Westminster. It was not a vital concession from England's point of view and indeed in some ways it left the Irish worse off than they were before in that they no longer had the wholehearted support of the Church, but it taught them a valuable lesson in political organization.

Some of them took the lesson to be that power flows from the barrel of a gun, and formed themselves into Mafia-like terrorist secret societies, but the less aggressive tried to exert influence on the Establishment in other ways. Justice was not to be expected between landlord and tenant, but mercy could often be obtained by plausible cajolery. Blarney became a survival characteristic. Flattery was augmented by favors and bribes, so that a magistrate who was to try a case would get his first news of it in the form of unexpected gifts and services, the donors sometimes not finding it necessary to "put in a word," so well was the system understood. A network of favors and obligations covered the country, and a man in trouble cashed in his stock. If he was unsuccessful he assumed his bid in the auction had not been high enough, and set himself to extend his circle of allies. Sometimes a magistrate would in effect be brought by one faction, and become their protector, and they his servants. To the Irish the figure of English justice had both eyes open, a thumb on the scales, and the other hand outstretched, palm upwards.

Pioneers in political organization, cynical about political ideals, experts in persuasion and personal relationships: four million people like this, knit together by suffering and desperate for security, were injected into the bloodstream of America at a critical stage in its growth. Having learned in Ireland that they could not beat City Hall, in America they joined it.

John Kennedy's political advisors were called O'Donnell, O'Brien, Donahue and Dungan, while his academic brain-trust bore names like Sorenson, Schlesinger, Feldman and Rostow. It was a significant indication of how the source of Irish-American political strength had hindered their own progress, so that for generations they wandered blindly through the undergrowth of American politics, like a Samson with his hair over his eyes. They joined the Democratic Party because the Federalists had taken the side of England during the Napoleonic Wars. They brought the other ethnic minorities in with them, leading them by virtue of their greater political sophistication and knowledge of the language; but while the other minorities moved upwards into middle-class America the Irish remained in the role they had found for themselves, the professional bridesmaids of American politics.

Unskilled and more destitute than any Europeans, they had begun their life in America as "white niggers," with all that the epithet implied. But soon they made virtues of their necessities. To leave the ghettoes was disloyal, to improve one's living standards was suspect. Poverty was ascetic, spiritual. Wealth was materialistic, Protestant, English, evil. Their Church encouraged them to stay in their ghettoes where it could keep an eye on them and preserve their educational segregation. Eventually the shanty Irish became the "lace curtain Irish," once defined by Fred Allen as "people who have fruit in the house when no one is sick," but it took a hundred years for one of them to reach the top. John Kennedy had countered the ghetto problem by sending his sons to non-Catholic schools, and outside the ghettoes the Irish made it on their own. Nowadays it seems that whatever the party you have to look hard to find a presidential candidate who is not of Irish descent.

Whatever the Irish did for, or to, the politics of America, they did much to humanize its government. They saw the problems of administration as the problems of individual people, which is a rare and excellent quality in a bureaucrat. What seemed like corruption and nepotism to Protestant reformers was to them a way of adapting situations to people rather than people to situations. Their complex system of reciprocal favors was generally practiced with its own integrity, and suffused with a human warmth which must have done much to reassure the poor that someone cared about them. Their attitude was personified in the genial Irish cop of folklore, solving the human problems of his beat in his own pragmatic unofficial way.

The good Irish policeman was a living proof of Plato's contention that the only people who should be allowed to wield power are those who do not want it. This is a view subconsciously accepted in Britain, where a candidate "stands," as opposed to America, where he "runs," and there is something to be said for the argument that the desire to have power over people is the worst qualification to be given it. Certainly the Irish did not become policemen for that reason, but simply because it was a Government job for which no special qualifications were required. When a starving man has been fed, his next thought is to make sure of his next meal, and in a peasant this is translated into a longing for the possession of land and the security it affords. But the

Irish had not owned land for many generations, and to them it meant only insecurity and famine. The only security open to them was Government employment, and they seized on it with all the avidity of a landless peasant taking possession of a field. Even back in Ireland, women admiring a new baby would say, "God bless the fine boy. Sure it's a fine post office sorter he'll make when he grows up."

Altogether it seems very appropriate that the White House should have been designed by a Kilkenny architect and modeled after Leinster House in Dublin, home of the old Irish Parliament. The Irish made their mark in so many other fields that it would be almost easier to list the prominent Americans who do not have Irish ancestry. Much the same applies in Canada, with added complications evidenced by such facts that at the battle for Quebec, which determined the future of the country, the generals on both sides were Irish.

To the south, eighty thousand Irish women and children sold into slavery by Cromwell added a touch of brogue to the calypso. In Cuba they remember the great Governor General Marshal Leopold O'Donnell of Spain, later conqueror of Morocco, Duke of Tetuan and Prime Minister. In Argentina they remember that their navy was founded by an Admiral Brown, a man from Mayo. An Irishman called O'Higgins became Viceroy of Peru. Another O'Higgins was the liberator of Chile, and became its first president.

The Irish connection with South America grew largely from the fact that some of the Wild Geese were horses. (This is an authentic, newly created Irish Bull.) The limestone soil and mild climate of Ireland had made its horses famous throughout Europe for centuries. Napoleon's famous white horse Marengo was bred at Kilmuckbridge, County Wexford; and they say that at Waterloo Wellington was mounted on a black stallion bought at Cahirmee in County Cork, which was one of the biggest horse fairs in Europe. Many Irishmen followed their horses to the pampas of South America and many came back prosperous, so that they say you could hear Spanish spoken in the lanes of Meath.

But in the United States most immigrants took the cold turkey cure for homesickness, and few came back to the old country. Those who did found it had changed less than they. The listlessness and fecklessness which had convinced England that the Irish were unfit for self-government had dropped away completely, revealing brisk, confident Irish-Americans. The change in the immigrants was so sudden that one is driven to the conclusion that it was due to the replacement of something that had been missing from their diet—probably food.

The emigrants that did return were viewed by the old Irish with a mixture of awed admiration and tolerant contempt, and their new ideas were not always welcome. In his book *Ireland and the American Emigration*, Arnold Schrier tells of a woman who came back rich from America to the tiny hamlet where she was born and proposed to put a slate roof on the cottage her old brothers still lived in. This daring idea was reluctantly accepted, but when she went on to suggest that a bedroom might be built on while they were at it, that was another story. "By God," said her brother, aghast at such a grandiloquent conception, "you're not going to make another New York out of Ballyfad!"

10. The Old Country

The way of life in Ireland changed little until after 1920, and lingers on in many places, not least, I suspect, in the minds of Irish-Americans. Green hills and brown bogs lie among blue mountains, dotted with tiny white thatched cottages. From each chimney a lazy spiral of smoke fills the air with the unforgettable fragrance of the turf fire, that distinctive half-forgotten smell of Ireland which catches at the heart of a returning exile. I have often thought that if you were to release a cloud of peat smoke over the United States a tenth of the population would burst into tears. Eventually some enterprising manufacturer will market it, in what I suppose he will call eiresols.

The long memories of the Irish, which the English criticize so much, are those of a people with a great love of learning deprived of the means of recording it, and who have lost everything except their identity. That identity would have been lost without the continuity of the Irish home, where for centuries love and warmth kept alive the memories of Ireland. The true symbol of Ireland is not the shamrock, or even the harp but the turf fire.

No matter how poor a family was, there was always warmth in the home, a place for the family to unite and for tales to be told. The turf was there for the cutting in the bogs, the legacy of the great forests that covered Ireland when Man first found it. It is dark brown, fibrous, light to carry and clean to handle, and it burns evenly without flame. In every respect it is superior to coal as a solid domestic fuel, except that it is bulky. Nowadays it is gathered by great machines and used to fuel huge power stations nearby, the only ones of their kind in the world outside Russia, or compressed into neat briquettes for sale in supermarkets, stamped *BnM* for Bord na Mona, the state Turf Board. But there are still places where the men cut it with long thin spades and leave the brown bricks to dry in the sun, and the children trot barefoot through the bog cotton with tea from the house.

As long as the family had a roof over their heads, the fire never went out. The fine ash has the insulating qualities of asbestos, and a shovelful on the fire keeps it in overnight. For cooking it was infinitely adaptable. A few embers, prepared from the smaller pieces of turf known as *kerauns*, would be spread on the stone hearth to be both hob and heat for a frying pan. Pots could be hung at varying heights from a great pivoted arm called the crane, fixed at one side of the hearth. At the other was often a wheel bellows. If there was an ingenious local blacksmith the degree of control exercisable over cooking on a turf fire rivaled that in a modern stove, and it was a lot less likely to go wrong.

For the poor the food was mostly potatoes, but even the poorest families often had a cow which they grazed on the grass verges of the road, known in those days as the Long Meadow. A plate of potatoes mashed with milk and chopped scallions, with a lump of melting butter on top, was a dish called *colcannon*, fit for a king.

When times were better the housewife baked a bewildering variety of bread, some of which—griddle wheaten, soda farls, potato bread—are still popular. I've heard that an enterprising immigrant in Toronto bakes them, and Irish-Canadians drive two hundred miles to buy them. On the coasts and near the rivers there was fish to be had in plenty. In Belfast apprentices insisted on it being written into their indentures that they were not to be given salmon more than twice a week. A form of seaweed called *dulse* is still sold as a delicacy in candy shops in the east. It tastes like solidified seawater. During the Famine the whole west coast was cleared of this seaweed.

Reading the history of Ireland it is hard to see how the life of the people could have held anything but misery and terror, but a man cannot worry about famine and eviction and the future all the time; as long as there was food and warmth, cheerfulness kept breaking in. Sir Walter Scott in 1825, though appalled at the poverty of the people, noticed that "their natural condition is turned towards gaiety and happiness."

There was horse racing, coursing, hurling, athletics, wrestling, jumping, football, handball, tug-of-war, road bowling and rounders. Hurling, a sort of anarchic hockey, said to be the fastest ball game in the world, is still a great national sport, with an international every year against America in New York. Gaelic football, said to be the origin of rugby football in England and of the form of it played in America, is now also highly organized. Road bowling, more like golf than bowls in that the aim is to cover the distance between one village and another with the fewest throws of a heavy iron ball, is still played along the now tarmacadamed *boreens* of Cork and Armagh, with lookouts for cars and the not too watchful police. Rounders, from which baseball evolved, is still popular among children.

This was also the heyday of the poteen trade, when the contest with the police was something between a game and a war. Kevin Danaher in *Ireland Long Ago* tells of one skirmish when a sergeant and constable found a twenty gallon keg of poteen in the loft of a County Mayo farmhouse. The sergeant sat on the evidence and sent the constable for reinforcements, steadfastly ignoring all distractions and noises from the women below. A couple of hours later four constables arrived to carry the keg away, but they were not needed because the keg was now mysteriously empty. The women below had carefully bored a hole in the ceiling and drawn off the poteen. As an added precaution they had then squirted up some kerosene to banish the odor of guilt.

Another vanished sport was faction fighting, a sort of team fencing with sticks, which survives only in the so-called shillelaghs sold to tourists. Despite the names of some of the teams, like the rival Three Year Olds and Four Year Olds of Limerick (names apparently commemorating an argument over a horse at a fair), it was a sport for strong men, and the champions were famous for their skill and strength. Many were able to disable an opponent with one tap and one, Seamus Mor Hartnett, was reputed to have squeezed water out of the head of a blackthorn that had been seasoning up a chimney for seven years.

On the west coast, which is all inlets and islands, life revolved around the *curragh*, the frail but seaworthy craft of prehistoric design which is made and used today because there is still nothing better. In 1907 a

French ship was wrecked on a reef in Mal Bay, in a sea too rough for the lifeboat. The crew of the wrecked ship launched a raft, but it was broken to pieces by the waves. The men of Quilty village then put to sea in six *curraghs* and rescued all the crew. The present church at Quilty was built with money subscribed afterwards in France.

These were the days when everyone in Dublin seemed to be a poet or a rebel and that bastion of the Establishment, Trinity College, was producing even more than its usual quota of both. There was also a brilliant rash of eccentrics, in that fine old Dublin tradition of Buck Whaley, who once walked to Jerusalem for a bet of ten thousand pounds and played handball against the Wailing Wall. There was Bird Flanagan, who rode a horse through the swing doors of the Gresham Hotel, and his principal rival, who appeared at the Fancy Dress Ball at Earlsfort Terrace Skating Ring in 1909 dressed as the Holy Ghost. Assisted by his two disciples he laid an egg the size of a rugby football before a scandalized mob chased him fluttering from the arena.

The first steeplechase in the world was run in 1752 in Cork, from Buttevant to Doneraile Church, and the Irish passion for horses has not abated. At the 1964 Olympic Three Day event, seven out of the eight horses in the two winning teams were Irish. Interviewed on British television about the Pope and the Pill, an Irish doctor said the Encyclical would widen the gulf between the priests and the people, but it would not weaken the attachment of the Irish to their religion. "They will always love God, as they always have," he said, adding wryly by way of illustration, "They love horse racing too." He probably had in mind the fact that a love of nature is inherent in the Irish. Of early Irish poetry, Kuno Meyer said that it occupied "a unique position in the literature of the world. To seek out and watch and love nature was given to no people so early and so fully as the Celt."

The Irish relationship with animals was summed up by Leonard Wibberley, when he pointed out that the English loved animals, but animals loved the Irish. The early Irish saints believed that good animals went to heaven, and their lives are full of stories about them. Irish sea birds visited St. Columba in exile, and his contemporary, Mo Chua, had a pet cock, mouse and fly as companions. The cock would keep him awake at his studies, the mouse would operate as a paperweight, and the fly would mark his place. They were all he had in the world, and when they died he bewailed his loss to Columba, who replied rather unsympathetically, "There is no misfortune except where wealth is." Another saint had a friendly deer who offered his antlers for a lectern. Another saint, who had prayed so long that a thrush nested on his outstretched hands, stayed in that position until the eggs hatched out. More recently Richard Martin of Connemara, remembered as "Humanity Martin," promoted at Westminster in 1822 the first act to be passed in any parliament in the world for the protection of animals. The modern equivalent of the immobile saint is presumably the Dublin construction company which hired an extra truck at two hundred dollars a week when their workers refused to disturb a bird which had nested on the tipping hinge of their own vehicle. (*The People,* June 16, 1968).

The Irish understanding with animals extended even to rats, it being widely believed that if you stood near their holes and told them of a place where they could find better accommodation and asked them politely to leave, they would do so. Some years ago *Collier's Magazine* reported this belief as being current in Maine, brought there by immigrants from Ulster.

After horses their main friends were dogs, and they are one of the few nations to have erected a statue to one. This is the statue of the greyhound Master Magrath, at Dungarvan, County Waterford. Master Magrath (pronounced *Magraw*) won the Waterloo Cup in England three times running (how else?), though perhaps not in quite so spectacular a style as is reported in the contemporary song:

The hare she led on with a wonderful view,
And swift as the wind o'er the green field she flew.
But he jumped on her back and he held up his paw—
"Three cheers for old Ireland," says Master Magrath.

Originally the national dog had been the Irish wolfhound, a huge animal so gentle and wise that the Irish used it as a domestic pet and for rounding up cattle, and so brave and strong that the Romans pitted it against lions in the arena, but it ate more than a man and its place was largely taken by the sheepdog. Some of these animals were so accomplished that Kevin Danaher in *Irish Country People* reports seeing a man being offered a hundred pounds for his dog, and refusing it. He also mentions a dog in his district which would run into the house and bring out a half-burned sod of turf in his teeth when his master wanted to light his pipe. Once when he was showing off this trick to visitors the dog seemed to have goofed off and the spectators began to express doubts. But the owner told them to wait and eventually the dog appeared with the burning turf, walking backwards in the wind to keep the sparks out of his eyes.

The Irish even remember St. Patrick's goat, and mourn the manner of its passing. According to the legend, St. Patrick had taken the goat with him on board ship while he was cruising down the east coast of Ireland, and near the town of Skerries he let it ashore for a bit of a rest and a graze. Unfortunately the people of Skerries found it and ate it, and they never been able to live this down. In Shanghai in the late 19th Century some Irish soldiers from the neighboring village of Rush drinking in a bar heard Skerries' voices from the other side of a partition, so one of them shouted over it, "Who ate the goat?" Pandemonium broke loose, the Chinese took sides, and the resultant riot took a week to quell.

Animals now appear on the Irish coinage, from a horse on the most valuable coin down through a salmon, a bull, a wolfhound, a hare, a hen and a pig to a woodcock. The Irish harp is the common symbol on the other side, and this fact has involved untold difficulties among children in Northern Ireland. Before the rest of Ireland became independent in 1921, the penny minted for Ireland had a harp on one side and the king's head on the other, so children tossing a coin called Head or Harp more often than Head or Tails. With the intense conservatism of children they still do this, so that a sufficiently ingenious and unscrupulous child can now win every toss by supplying a Republic of Ireland coin, very common in Northern Ireland, and calling Head. If it comes down with the animal uppermost he points out that its head is the only one on the coin, and the other is Harp, an open and shut case. But if the harp comes uppermost, he points out that this is the symbol common to all Free State coins, and therefore equivalent to an English head, and that the only tail on the coin belongs to the animal. An equally unanswerable argument, if delivered with sufficient assurance. No doubt it will be to the long-term benefit of the country if rewards are to accrue to the clever rather than to the lucky.

In the long twilight evenings, there was dancing on wooden platforms at the crossroads, and in farmhouse kitchens, and for the latter a type of singing was developed called lilting, to take the place of music.

Until gentility set in, and with it a mausoleum called a parlor, the kitchen was where visitors were entertained. "God save all here," you would say when you came in, and "God save you kindly," would be the reply. Then you would be sat down in the great hearth and anything of comfort in the house made available to you freely and with affection. Many things were lost in Ireland during her privations, but not her ancient tradition of hospitality. Sir Walter Scott found "perpetual kindness in the Irish cabin," and even in the worst days of the Famine itself, when people were dying in their thousands, "the poor Irish never refused admission to the poorest and most abject mendicant." The quotation comes from *The Great Hunger*, by Cecil Woodham-Smith, who also found the phenomenon officially recorded in a contemporary report of the Central Board of Health. "The Irishman thinks himself accursed if he refuses admission to a begging stranger."

Often in the old days the stranger would be a traveling storyteller, and even after they died out stories of the old days would be told around these fires, the children listening even if they were supposed to be asleep. To them gossip, history and legend were equally real.

The first duty of a child on some Irish farms is to feed the hens. He is told this is very important because the hens were brought to Ireland by the Norsemen, and first thing every morning when they wake up they remember this and make up their minds to go back home. This disaster must be averted by distracting their attention with breakfast. If it is delayed by a lazy child they will all flurry away to Norway and there will be no more eggs. On the other hand, if they are given food right away the foolish birds will forget again in their excitement and the situation will be saved for another day. It is perfectly obvious to any sensible child noting the urgency of cock crow, the bright-eyed purposefulness of hens emerging from their coop and their hysterical behavior over breakfast, that all this is perfectly true. And even if it isn't he is being given a pride in his work and a sense of its importance which will last him until he is able to understand more adult incentives.

Scientists now believe that the domestic fowl was in fact introduced into Ireland from Scandinavia, but to find value in a children's story is nothing strange in Ireland. When a schoolteacher was telling his class about how the Golden Gorget of Gillasheen had been found by a man walking his dog in the Burren, a little boy asked, "Was it anything like this?" and produced a priceless gold fibula he had found in the bog and was using as a toy.

Something like that schoolteacher's thrill was described by Iona and Peter Opie in their *Lore and Language of Schoolchildren*:

It is an exciting experience to walk into a school-room in one of the poorest quarters of Dublin and hear a nine year old urchin give this cryptic description of a maid milking a cow:

Ink ank under a bank

Ten drawing four

being already aware that this was how the riddle was posed in Charles I's time:

Clinke clanke under a banke

Ten above four and nearer the stanke

and being able to tell oneself that it was highly unlikely that the child, or any of his forebears, had ever seen these words in print, for during the centuries of the riddle's existence it has only been printed two or three times, in obscure places.

Children are the great custodians of tradition, and more often it is preserved by passage from child to child, and not through adults at all. Every one of us has a great store of childhood lore locked up in our subconscious along with all the other forgotten memories of our youth. An unexpected cue of a once-important word, like for instance "skate key," can unlock a door on a world of memory we didn't know existed. I wonder how many such doors the Clancy Brothers opened when they made a song out of the chant of little girls in one of their street games:

> *I'll tell my ma when I go home,*
> *The boys won't leave the girls alone,*
> *They pull my hair, they stole my comb,*
> *And that's all right till I go home.*
> *She is handsome, she is pretty;*

She is the belle of Belfast city,
She is courtin' one, two, three.
Please won't you tell me who is she?

Let the wind and the rain and the hail blow high
And the snow come traveling from the sky . . .
Let them all come as they will,
But 'tis Albert Mooney she loves still.

The long memory of children is instanced vividly in their game of Ring a Roses, which is believed to recall the Great Plague of the 17th Century. A pink rash like ringworm was the first symptom; people carried posies of flowers in the belief they warded off infection, a custom which survives in English law courts; "tishoo tishoo" is the sneezing of the victims; and fall down was what hundreds of thousands of them did in that terrible winter.

There is a short story by Eric Linklater which has the same wonderment. It is a straightforward account of an interview with an old sailor whose family had been sea-faring folk for generations and had handed down stories of their adventures. The journalist, listening with half an ear to yet another interminable tale, abruptly realizes with awe that what he is now hearing is part of the Odyssey, an eye-witness account of Jason's voyage in search of the Golden Fleece by a member of his crew.

Ireland can be like that. As Elizabeth Bowen put it, "to travel in Ireland is to travel some way back in time." It is obvious at once to the most casual visitor, in such things as the inaccuracy of public clocks and the absence of nagging time signals on the radio, that in this timeless land there is time for everything. And then it becomes clear that the past too is part of this timeless present, not just preserved but living.

I once heard an Irishman dismiss American history as a mere collection of newspaper clippings, referring to its quantity rather than its quality. Eight thousand years of history can fill a small country like Ireland to overflowing with memories. It is as if every tiny creek in America had all the emotional significance of the Delaware or the Alamo, and the events associated with it the same importance to the present life of the people. But in other countries history is safely buried in books, while in the Irish village a child will see every day a prehistoric dolmen, a Celtic cross, a ruined castle, a tumbled-down cottage and a burned-out mansion, and he will know what all these mean. Furthermore his knowledge will not have been gathered and processed in universities, but home grown, so that he will know familiar fields to be places where the Fianna fought, or Cromwell killed, or Patrick preached or Dermod and Grania slept. The history of his country is part of his life, and without realizing this no one can know what it is like to wake up in the morning and say to oneself with surprise and pleasure and a certain sadness, I am Irish.

11. The Word

If you should ever come home from work to find a pile of stones in your hearth with an eggshell full of water on top, run do not walk to your friendly neighborhood exorcist. An Irish curse has been laid on you, known as the Fire of Stones. It means, "May you never have luck, until this fire of stones boils this water."

I'm not sure what the equivalent is for central heating installations, but it does not do to assume that modern equipment is immune from curses, or so it would seem from the contest between Tory Island and the British Navy. This island, which from the coast of Donegal looks rather like a battleship itself, used to be a fortress of the Fomorians: King Balor lived there in a glass castle, which he had built to increase the effective range of his personal armament, a single eye which could strike people dead just by looking at them. Ever since then the people of Tory had considered themselves independent of Ireland, never mind England, and declined to pay taxes. In 1884 the British government followed the precedent for dealing with situations like this by sending a gunboat, the HMS *Wasp;* the people of Tory turned the Cursing Stones against it. There were about fifty-one of these Cursing Stones, though it was said you got a different number every time you tried to count them, a thing that often happens to me with ordinary objects. By turning each of them around anti-clock-wise the power of a curse was considerably amplified. Anyway, the HMS *Wasp* ran onto the rocks and all but six of the crew were drowned, an outcome which can have done little to disillusion the Tory Islanders from their foolish superstitions.

This belief in the power of words and symbols existed even in worldly Dublin, and sometimes took the oddest forms. Once it actually imperiled such a fundamental of Irish well-being as the sales of Guinness, according to Lynch and Vaizey's scholarly work on the place of that brewery in the Irish economy. The Guinness family were Protestants, and the early 19th Century was a time of bitter religious controversy. In 1813 a Dr. Brennan made the startling disclosure that these brewers of "anti-popery porter" had been in the practice of mashing up Protestant Bibles and Methodist hymnbooks in their vats, impregnating their product with the essence of Protestantism and inducing innocent Catholics to swallow, literally, these heretical doctrines. Some 136,000 tons of Bibles and 501,000 cartloads of hymnbooks had been used in this diabolical way, the good doctor went on with devastating detail. However, he was helpful enough to add that Pim's ale fortunately offered a complete antidote.

This classic piece of knocking copy was solemnly refuted by the authorities, but it affected the sales of Guinness for some little time. It may be, of course, that many customers were put off by the idea of drinking ink and paper, of whatever religion, but there is surely some significance in the fact that the story was published at all.

One of the more engaging characteristics of the early Irish was that they apparently believed in Continuous

Creation, if not quite according to Hoyle. In the *Annals of the Four Masters,* which purport to set out the history of Ireland from the landing of Cesair, granddaughter of Noah, in the Year of the World 2242, we are continually being told that in such and such a year this and that well-known lake or river "sprang forth." This fascinating picture of the world as a large stage set, in which new props are constantly appearing, was typical of Irish philosophy. If the physical world is illusory and impermanent, thoughts must then be the true reality: and words, being thoughts made manifest, must be symbols of special power. The first words of the Christian Bible, "In the beginning was the Word," must have seemed to the Druids to be an expression of one of their own profoundest beliefs.

It followed that craftsmen in words had special importance in Celtic society. To rank as a great warrior a man had to be able to utter a telling gibe as well as a deadly blow, and poets ranked even higher than the warriors. Not only were they the ancient equivalent of newspapers and television, with all the power those media have today, they were believed to have magic powers inherent in their craft, so that a man could actually be killed by a deadly satire and his posterity withered by a curse. Poets were therefore greatly respected, and well paid for their work. One of them reports having been given twenty horned cows for one poem, a word rate most modern authors would envy.

As time went on, however, the poets became so numerous and so indolent as to constitute a nuisance. In fact the country was suffering from a plague of beatniks. King Aedh called a conference of nobles to discuss banishing the lot of them, and they were only saved by the dramatic intervention of St. Columba, who had gone into exile after the Battle of the Books, pledging never to set foot or lay eyes on Ireland again. He founded a monastery on the Scottish island of Iona, as near to Ireland as it is possible to be without being in sight of it. In exile he had acquired such a reputation for wisdom that he was asked to advise on the bard question, and he came back to Ireland to do so. Standing blindfold on a sod brought from Iona he advised the bards to reform themselves and the king to confine himself to limiting their numbers, and this compromise was accepted.

Since then the thought has occasionally occurred to many people that St. Columba was too easy on the bards, and that their successors still have too great power in Ireland. In 1809 a wandering poet called O'Kelly wrote a ballad called "The Curse of Doneraile," a savage indictment of that town occasioned by the fact that somebody there had stolen his gold watch. The poem became so famous that the tradesmen of the town began to fear for their livelihood, and petitioned Lady Doneraile to do something about it. She bought the poet another gold watch and he wrote another ballad, "In Praise of Doneraile," which unfortunately never quite caught up with the first one.

O'Kelly had particularly prized his gold watch because it had been given to him by George IV of England. With the traditional effrontery of bards he had contrived to be presented to the King, representing himself to be a great national poet, like Byron and Scott. Amused, George IV asked how he thought he compared with those two, and O'Kelly extemporized the following:

Three poets for three sister kingdoms born.
One for the Rose, another for the Thorn;
One for the Shamrock which never will decay,
While Rose and Thistle yearly fade away.

In handing out a gold watch for this instead of an indictment for treason, George IV was following the example of earlier magnanimous monarchs confronted with such impudence, like Charlemagne. He had as one of his principal confidantes the Irish scholar Eriugena, also known as Scotus, Irishmen in those days being called Scots. The two were drinking together one evening when the Emperor, feeling that Eriugena had had a bit too much, asked unkindly how far was a Scot removed from a sot. The reply, "the width of a table," was bright enough to save Scotus from summary execution and indeed earned him a sort of popular immortality, without doing Charlemagne's reputation any harm. This is supposed to have been the first joke of modern Europe. One cannot help wondering how many other Irish wits between Charlemagne and George IV may have perished for the sake of a jest which died with them.

Kings were quite right to fear poets and wits, because they could visit on them a fate worse than death. A thoughtful king, knowing that his reputation will live after him, must value it more than his life, and realize how likely it is that all his work might be forgotten in favor of a single illuminating incident or casual remark. Something like this happened to the unfortunate James II, who lost his throne at the Battle of the Boyne and his reputation in Dublin shortly afterwards. Fleeing from the battlefield, he burst in on Lady Tyrconnell crying, "Those scoundrels of Irishmen ran!" "Indeed?" said Lady Tyrconnell sweetly; "I see your Majesty won the race."

Politicians are almost as vulnerable today, of course, and everyone can think of examples. Only the language barrier saved Khruschev after a Dublin columnist had nicknamed him Fatsy Pagan. By poetic justice, poets themselves are equally vulnerable: the mystical verse of a famous bearded poet has never seemed quite the same since another author dubbed him the Hairy Fairy.

Writers are vulnerable creatures armed with deadly weapons they cannot resist using, and the carnage in Irish literary circles is at times dreadful to behold. An Irish literary movement was defined as three writers in the same town who all hate one another. Even outside those circles, the apparent malice of the Irish is very disturbing to strangers. The Englishman who comes to live in Dublin is first delighted with the kindness and friendliness of everyone; then one day he hears what his friends are saying behind his back, and is terribly hurt, and goes home again dismissing the Irish as deceitful and treacherous. But their friendliness was not insincere. It is just that when they conceive a good joke they view the prospect of not giving it birth with the same moral repugnance their Church feels to abortion.

This applied even in the case of a man as kindly as Father Healy, who acquired a great reputation as a wit in his day. Most of the examples which have come down to us seem unfortunately to be of the "you ought to have been there" variety. The American authoress Mrs. T. P. O'Connor, whose book *Herself Ireland* reflects with equal enthusiasm her love for her adopted country, her admiration for Father Healy and her addiction to gravy, gives several pages of instances of the good Father's "continual quickness of wit," but I think one is enough. Asked was he *au fait* with the French language he replied, "No, I am only O'Healy at it."

Now that you have picked yourself off the floor I might direct your attention to the kindly and amiable Father Healy visiting the deathbed of another priest, who had been his rival for a long time. Recounting the touching scene later, Father Healy said that "he brushed a tear from his rough cheek" but was unable to resist adding that it seemed to have been "the only thing that had been brushed in the room for years."

This natural irreverence of the Irish has a profound effect on the public life of the country. Pompous ritual such as is so popular in England is impossible in Ireland for fear of ridicule; politicians are careful to be unpretentious enough to evade satire, and flamboyant oratory is avoided in the certain knowledge that the emotional peroration will be punctured by a pointed comment from a heckler. The eloquent oratory of the Irish is a myth except in law, where the enforced silence of the audience enables the courts to become battlegrounds of emotional advocacy, and here eloquence is indeed admired by all. A professional murderer being tried for his life in a famous case was so overcome by admiration for the eloquence of the prosecuting counsel that he exclaimed to the warder standing beside him in the dock: "I don't give a damn what anyone says, that's the best bloody speech ever, and that bit about the innocent blood calling from the earth was the best of all."

Political eloquence is usually confined to the rare instances where the entire audience is at one with the speaker. Even in America the average Irish politician was a committee man rather than a demagogue, and eschewed flamboyance in dress or behavior. In Ireland itself it is difficult to get people to speak at meetings, and the real controversy is carried on in pubs afterwards and in the correspondence columns of newspapers. An English stage hypnotist had to cut short a vaudeville tour in Ireland through shortage of volunteers to come on the stage. Generally speaking, the average Irishman is diffident and quiet spoken, eloquent only among small groups of friends.

This national diffidence is no doubt partly due to a lack of confidence resulting from centuries of subjection, but it is not helped by the national talent for mockery and ridicule, and the knowledge that a joke against one will be told and retold with delight, to hang around one's neck for life like a curse. In the Belfast *Telegraph* there are sometimes features reporting such caustic comments, the local equivalent of the *Reader's Digest* department "Towards More Picturesque Speech":

Her legs are like matchsticks with the wood scraped off.
The foreman sent him to the hospital for an X-ray, to see if there's any trace of work left in him.
The mother that reared him would drown nothing.
With yon buck teeth he could eat a tomato through a tennis racket.
Her honeymoon was just a busman's holiday.

More recently the average Irishman has appeared in television interviews, sometimes with equal impact. Recently a firm in Derry closed down following disputes, throwing many people out of work. An old woman whose three sons were now unemployed seemed disposed to be critical of the conduct of the owner, and the interviewer pointed out that he was worried about the situation too. "The difference between us," said the old woman, quietly but devastatingly, "is that he does his worrying in the Bahamas."

12. The Old Sow That Eats its Own Farrow

"The cup of Ireland's misfortunes has been overflowing for centuries," said Sir Boyle Roche, "and it is not full yet." Not for the first time, the old gentleman had hit the nail unerringly on the thumb.

When Ireland was finally rid of the English, to whom all its troubles had been conveniently attributable, it observed with some surprise that it had not immediately blossomed into a Celtic Utopia, all cut-glass and poetry. Instead the Irish themselves seemed to be rushing into the vacuum left by the English and to be inflicting further misfortunes on the unfortunate country. The apparent tendency of the Irish to destroy their own fondest hopes led one of them despairingly to refer to his motherland as "the old sow that eats its own farrow," a typically extreme reaction. It seems to me that Ireland faces a litter problem in quite another sense, the problem of disposing of the rubbish of the past.

The visitor notices it most in places like Clifden, Connemara. It is a town which reminds me of Jacksonville,

Florida, though I imagine the two places could hardly be less alike. I have never seen Jacksonville, Florida, but somebody told me once that the countryside thereabouts is so extremely flat that the local council constructed a hill in the town park so that the children could see what one is like. Similarly, parts of Clifden are obviously designed to show the local children what ugliness is like, it being a phenomenon no child would otherwise have a chance of seeing in Connemara. The effect has been cleverly and economically obtained by introducing a little garbage into the exquisite bay, where it moves majestically backwards and forwards with the tide, and by placing larger collections of it in strategic positions about the town. Thanks to the ingenuity of modern manufacturers, who have removed all the durable qualities from their products and incorporated them in the wrappings, the result is a memorial to the people of Clifden as permanent as the mountains which surround them.

The same explanation cannot be offered for many other villages in Ireland, which are ugly enough in themselves without help. Compared with the pretty old-world English villages, some are a depressing sight. Part of the trouble is that the Irish have not been able to afford prettiness and have had to put up with beauty, which God has given them free. It takes money to build good houses in the first place, and to keep them in repair century after century, and to buy the machines or the time needed to trim hedges and grass verges, and to build good fences and gate posts and put those little English metal caps on them to keep the rain from entering the end grain. But the visitor, vexed by the contrast between the beautiful country and the ugly village, cannot help wondering why the people cannot get together for a few hours and render at least some first aid to the eyesore in which they live.

Then there is the delicate question of hygiene. I hesitate to use the word "dirt" because it implies that a fine piece of home-cured Limerick ham, exposed to the forces of nature as it has been since it was a pig, is somehow inferior to a processed food imprisoned in polythene along with a lot of strange chemicals which for all you know may cause your grandchildren to be born with two heads. Nevertheless, standards of hygiene in shops are lower than many visitors today expect.

And yet the ancient Celts had very high standards of hygiene. The Brehon Laws, for example, required hospitals to have four open doors and a stream of water running through, anticipating modern codes of hospital ventilation by some two thousand years.

Part of the reason for all this is that the Irish are essentially a rural people, and country people are the last to be trusted with the preservation of the countryside or to worry about a bit of what they call good clean dirt. The average farmer notices scenery no more than we notice air, and a man who is close to the soil will usually have some of the soil close to him. As for litter, it may be that the Irish are no worse than most people; it's just that a small country is more vulnerable to desecration. I dare say you could drop a thousand tons of garbage into the Grand Canyon without making it any less impressive, but a single plastic carton can ruin a stretch of west Ireland coast for the sort of people who like the west of Ireland. (A bottle isn't so bad, because you can persuade yourself it had a message in it from some shipwrecked mariner.)

There still remains the mysterious matter of Irish food. The grass is so rich in the dairy lands of Ireland that the cows have frequently to be treated for dyspepsia, and produce the sort of milk described by a Gaelic poet: "yellow bubbling milk, the swallowing of which needs chewing, milk that sounds like the snoring bleat of a ram as it rushes down the throat." And yet in hotels it is rare to be served cream with one's cornflakes or coffee, and not unheard of to be offered—no, given—some synthetic substitute for whipped cream with dessert; and too often the dessert is canned or frozen, even in the middle of the strawberry season, as are the soups and vegetables. Once I was even served with tinned potatoes. I put it to the manager of this blighted establishment, when I discovered he was not going to be lynched, that a visitor to Ireland might reasonably expect to be served with fresh Irish food. He launched into a dissertation on the problems of bulk buying, ending with the bland statement that the future of hotel catering lay in the use of canned and frozen foods entirely.

This wretched man was under the illusion that he ran a first-class hotel, and had assurances to this effect from several organizations and many of his guests. The organizations seem to be interested only in plumbing, apparently under the impression that people spend their holidays in the bathroom, and the guests were either too diffident to complain or did not know there was anything to complain about. The general standard of Irish domestic cookery is so low that people think anything served out of a silver dish is *haute cuisine.* But you would think that a hotel manager with any pride in his hotel would encourage the local farmers and their wives to set up market gardens under contract to the hotel. It seems no one can be bothered.

The fecklessness and apathy of the Irish in the 19th Century convinced many Englishmen that the people were incapable of self-government; yet in Elizabethan times an English writer had described them as "of paines infinite, sharpe-witted, lovers of learning, capable of any studie whereunto they bende themselves, constant in travaile."

For a clue to what happened we could have stayed in Clifden and looked up the minutes of the Guardian of the Workhouse. We would have found such entries as this:

Nov. 18, 1848. There died this day at the Gates 240 souls.

In her shattering book, *The Great Hunger,* Cecil Woodham-Smith describes a country laid waste, a civilization in ruins and a people reduced to lower than the level of beasts. Even in Dublin, which escaped the worst of the Famine by reason of its economy being part of that of England, shops in the finest streets had their shutters up, and broken windows stuffed with paper. Trade all over Ireland had virtually ceased, even farming had ended over vast areas, and the people who used to till the soil had either died or emigrated, or were left wandering the country as diseased and starving beggars.

Nor had this disaster—or these disasters, for there were several famines—struck a people who had the energy and will to recover. Deprived of education and debased by the law for generations, the best of every generation gone abroad, trapped in a system of land ownership which penalized hard work and enterprise, their standard of living already the lowest in Europe, their situation had been hopeless before the Famine.

However, the famines struck the death blow. When the first soup kitchens were set up, the Irish had still enough pride and dignity to resent standing in line to be fed like animals; the people of Newmarket-on-Fergus, County Clare, petitioned that the method of distribution "debases and demoralizes," and elsewhere in the county a boiler was actually overturned. But towards the end they were kneeling to landowners in the streets. During the famines themselves the Irish preserved their generous tradition of hospitality, but in the typhus epidemic that followed even the bonds of family life were broken. The last vestiges of old decency had gone.

When one considers that all this happened in the lifetime of the parents of Irish people now living, it is clear that the most remarkable thing about the present-day Irish is their energy and enterprise. From where they started and with what they had, it is arguable that they have made more progress than any other Europeans. But a way of life is slow to change, especially in a people with long memories, and the spirit of the past still walks.

The system of land tenure made hard work unprofitable, even dangerous, and the potato made it unnecessary. A man did all his farming in a few weeks and spent the rest of his time talking or drinking or playing games. Some of this way of life persists today. As a city boy I used to think that farmers collapsed in exhaustion at sunset and got up at the scrake of dawn to milk the cows or something. But any time I have been on an

Irish farm they seem to whoop it up till two in the morning and lie in like actresses. I suppose the cows have got used to it. As for the farms themselves, I suppose one shouldn't say anything about them because the farmers are so amiable about your walking through them, but some of them are spectacularly untidy. Every old iron bedstead in the world seems to have found its eternal rest as part of a fence, and the improvised devices of twisted wire which take the place of hinges and bolts on gates are masterpieces of misplaced ingenuity. Even in the cities, tradesmen never come when they promised and your car is seldom ready in time at the garage.

No doubt this is partly due to the Irish decision to opt out of the rat race, which makes the country such a pleasant place to visit. But when you live there, immobilized in your house eating Danish butter and listening to the rain coming through the roof, you realize that Ireland's problem is to reconcile the human priorities of its way of life with the efficiency required for a 20th Century civilization.

Irish food is the best in the world, when you can get it, and when it survives Irish cooking. It was the potato that made a lost art of Irish cuisine. It swept through Irish kitchens like a deluge, as Father Mathew put it, sweeping into oblivion all the women's knowledge of cookery. What cottage recipes did survive were voluntarily abandoned along with the other relics of poverty, the housewife believing, for example, that her delicious home-baked bread must be inferior to the status symbol of the white loaf bought in the shop. This sort of snobbery persists today—in modern Belfast, people who have moved up in the world are still referred to as having "gone all pan loaf"—and the battle against it is being waged by the tourists. The peculiar result is that you can now get food in the very expensive hotels which would be looked down on by some of the native middle-class customers of the medium price hotels.

The battle against these complacent establishments, with their canned potatoes, frozen strawberries and plastic cream, is being fought by an alliance of younger Irish people and tourists, who patronize instead farmhouses advertising bed and breakfast. There they encourage the housewife to supply home-grown food, and this revival of Irish cookery is proving so profitable that the hoteliers are getting alarmed. The last I heard they were asking the Government to do something about this unfair competition, and I hope it refuses. I would like that man who told me that the future of Irish hotel catering lay in providing second rate food to realize that his future lies in the Bankruptcy Court.

These outworn attitudes are parts of the litter from the past that strike the tourist's eye, but there are plenty more. In the north, Protestant fundamentalists, wielding a hatchet that should have been buried long ago, are unconsciously chopping away with their backswing at the English connection they are trying to preserve. In the south, the fundamentalist Catholics, in trying to protect their young people from sin, are driving them into the godless cities and out of the church. And the heirs to the poets of the Easter Rebellion banished the writers of Ireland with their censorship, oblivious to the fact that as Arland Ussher pointed out, "it is seldom true of living organisms that they are improved by having their brains extracted."

These people are not ill-intentioned, and some of

them are not even stupid; their brains are simply asleep under a pile of old garbage. "History," said Stephen Daedalus, "is a nightmare from which we are trying to awake." In Ireland too many people have not yet heard the alarm clock.

13. When Irish Smiles are Lying

An Irish attorney was making his best of a rather shaky case when the judge interrupted him on a point of law. "Surely," he asked, "your clients are aware of the doctrine *de minimis non curat lex?*" "I assure you, my lord," came the suave reply, "that in the remote and inhospitable hamlet where my clients have their humble abode, it forms the sole topic of conversation."

It is appropriate that through an odd quirk of fate the author of Baron Munchausen should lie in Killarney Churchyard, for the Irish are great tellers of stories, though not always of lies intended to deceive.

Their deceitfulness has, however, been often remarked on by the English. Even Anthony Trollope, who had so many nice things to say about the Irish, found them "perverse, irrational and but little bound by the love of truth." Curiously enough this is a fault which has recurred with distressing frequency among the subject peoples of the English, and one must feel every sympathy with them in their continued misfortune. It might be of some consolation to them to reflect that their ill luck is shared by some of the nobler animals like the lion, who are often deceived by the shifty camouflage of the zebra.

It cannot be expected that human beings should be less resourceful than animals in ways of self-preservation—certainly not a people as resourceful in the manipulation of words as the Irish. The struggle between English law and Irish ingenuity is one of the classic conflicts of all time, reminiscent from one point of view of David taking on Goliath, and from another of Laocoon in the coils of the serpents.

In 19th Century law courts in Ireland the art of perjury reached hitherto undreamed of heights. Indeed it was organized into something like a science, and certain types of defense came to be recognized by the names of the Irish counties in which they had been perfected. There was, for example, the Kerry alibi. Since there is only one truth but falsehood is infinite, most false alibis are broken down by cross-examining the witnesses separately on points of detail they may have overlooked in preparing their stories, such as what kind of hat the accused was wearing when he was supposed to have been seen twenty miles away from the crime. The Kerry alibi circumvented this difficulty by being true in every detail but one, that one being the date. The witnesses would simply select a day on which they had seen the accused in that place at that time, so that they had only one lie to defend.

The Kerry alibi, however, had the disadvantage that it put all the accused's eggs in one basket, since he could not claim both that he was twenty miles away at the time and that there were extenuating circumstances. So an even deadlier weapon was devised, which became known as the Tipperary alibi. This took the form of swearing a Kerry alibi not for the accused, but for the main prosecution witness. It would be testified that he was twenty miles away at the time and so could not possibly have seen the crime. Not only did this have the advantage of preserving the accused's second line of defense, it could be detonated under the prosecution without warning, completely demolishing their case.

The most impudent and sophisticated example of these techniques was at Cork Assizes, in a prosecution for an attack on a landlord during the Land War. To everyone's astonishment the defense called only one witness, and that a prominent land agent. The defending counsel asked him did he remember the events of last Tuesday, 4th October, the date of the crime, and the land agent said he did. He reluctantly admitted that last Tuesday he had seen the accused a great distance away from the scene of the crime. In the ·face of this unimpeachable evidence the case was dismissed, an outcome which astounded even the defense counsel. Thinking over the case that evening he remembered that in his brief the client's lawyer had been strangely insistent that his first question should take the exact form, "Do you remember Tuesday, the 4th October last?" He looked at his diary and the missing piece of the puzzle fell into place. The 4th October had been a Wednesday.

Against such exquisite economy of effort the police were helpless, but they fought valiantly against the more cumbersome armaments of the normal Kerry and Tipperary alibis, where they were on their own ground. In each Royal Irish Constabulary station there were kept careful records of every fair, wedding, funeral, wake, party or other public function, in the hope of trapping some witness who would claim to have been at that place at that time. And often, being Irish themselves, the police gave as good as they got in the witness box. Once a judge was so surprised at the evidence given by a sergeant that he murmured, "It reminds me of the observation of Tacitus, *Omne ignotum pro magnifico*." (Meaning, everything unknown is wonderful.) Unruffled, the sergeant said, "Your Lordship has took the words out of my mouth."

This state of affairs was of course well understood by the legal profession in Ireland, who apparently enjoyed the battle of wits. The same judge who discharged a prisoner "without any stain on your character other than having been acquitted by a Limerick jury," once addressed another Limerick litigant as follows:

Look here, sir, tell me no more unnecessary lies. Such lies as your attorney advised you are necessary for the presentation of your fraudulent case I will listen to, though I shall decide against you whatever you swear, but if you tell another unnecessary lie I will put you in the dock.

However, when an English judge came up against the phenomenon he was aghast. This happened to Mr. Justice Darling in a case involving the identity of a valuable picture, when a cloud of Irish witnesses came to London to testify. The judge listened to their evidence with growing dismay, and finally asked one witness sternly: "In your country, what happens to a witness who does not tell the truth?" "Begor, my Lord," came the unusually honest reply, "I think his side usually wins."

147

Maurice Healy, from whose charming *Tales of the Munster Circuit* most of these stories come, attributes to the Irish witness the comparative failure in Ireland of Edward Carson, who later became such a great advocate in England. Healy points out that the remorseless cross-examination by which Carson made his English reputation would simply not have worked in Ireland. The average English witness was awed by the majesty of the law and concerned only to placate it. An awkward question would reduce him to a tongue-tied and apparently furtive silence, during which the implications intended by the cross-examiner would march unimpeded across the jury's minds and take up commanding positions. Whereas the same question to an Irish witness would have produced an incredulous request for it to be repeated, followed by an impassioned appeal to the judge for protection and then a profusion of irrelevant information, all of which time the witness was putting to good use to devise his eventual answer.

In fact the court was regarded by the Irish witness as something between a stage and an arena, and he came prepared to do battle with every weapon at his disposal, even one as insidious as the truth. Healy instances the case of a joiner who was asked about an event some time ago and replied that he couldn't remember but his mother had told him . . . At this point he was interrupted while the other side argued that such hearsay evidence was inadmissible. The witness followed it all with intelligent interest, knowing quite well the point at issue, but quite properly not interrupting. Finally it was decided that the witness' mother would have to be called and the witness was asked where she was. "I don't know," was the ingenuous reply; "she's been dead this thirty years."

This really comes into the category of practical jokes, of the type known in Ireland as codology. The best examples are a form of satire, in which the victim's failings bring about his own discomfiture, and from which the honest and unpretentious are immune. As W. C. Fields used to put it, you can't cheat an honest man.

The best recent example I know of was perpetrated by Belfastman Bob Shaw; there is a passing reference to it in his science fiction novel *The Two-Timers*. In the office where Bob used to work there was a man who didn't seem able to talk of anything else but the performance of his car, with which he drove everyone to distraction; in particular its economy in the use of gasoline. One felt that if he had driven it along the Golden Road to Samarkand for his holidays, his post cards back to the office would have consisted entirely of reports on mileage per gallon. And that if he improved the carburation any further, gasoline would have to be periodically pumped out of the tank. It was this last thought that inspired Bob to his diabolical ruse. The car was a small one, and parked in an alley behind the office. Bob began bringing a bottle of gasoline every morning and pouring it secretly into its tank. At first the owner was delighted with the improvement, and expatiated on it at great length. Almost incredible, he called it. So Bob began to increase the morning dose, quite gradually. The owner became more and more lyrical, though checking his calculations with increasing care. Then one morning, quite suddenly, he ceased to be able to believe what he was saying. Stopping abruptly in mid-sentence, he retired into a corner to think things over.

This is, in a way, a uniquely kindhearted type of practical joke, in that far from doing your victim any injury you give him a present. Crueler kinds are practiced in the grim industrial world of the Belfast shipyards, including one I quite hate to think of. When a new man begins work, they sometimes steal his pay packet out of his jacket. At lunchtime, when he discovers his loss, they all commiserate with him, except the one who is out at the city stores changing the notes in the pay packet into coin. During the afternoon they present these coins in a cap to the victim as being the result of a collection they have taken up among themselves, and his thanks are sometimes quite moving.

An equally cruel joke, but practiced on people who richly deserved it, was one by Sir Hugh de Lacy in the 11th Century. He had just brought about the downfall of his rival, the great Sir John de Courcy, by bribing the servants of that good man to give false evidence against their master, and they had come to him for what they called a "passport"; that is, a safe-conduct they could take with them to England as a sort of reference. Sir Hugh sent the illiterate traitors off with an imposing document he said they should produce any time they were in need of assistance. It read: "This writing witnesseth that those whose names are herein subscribed, that did betray a good master for reward, will be false to me and to all the earth besides."

A similarly imposing document, but one that has not yet been exposed, was created by our friend Bob Shaw when he was working in Canada. The transport manager in his firm prided himself on his sense of humor, evidenced by such witty pranks as bursting into the office to announce that the Russians had landed on the moon, and poking his head in again ten minutes later to add that they had found it was made of green cheese. He also thought he was very efficient, which was as true as his information about the moon. One day Bob, off work with a cold, found himself with both time on his hands and a sheet of the notepaper of a company which was one of the firm's customers. So he wrote the transport manager a letter purporting to be from the president of that company, congratulating him on the impeccable documentation with which his consignments arrived. Such dedicated efficiency had won his admiration and respect. If there were more men like the transport manager Canadian industry would soon out-distance the United States, etc. etc. Bob signed it *M. Bissell.*

He went back to work expecting that the joke would already have been traced to him. In Ireland suspicion would have set in with the first fulsome phrase, and even the giveaway signature would have been unnecessary. But to his alarm he found that his letter had already been photostated and copies distributed over half of Canada. Moreover, the original had already been expensively framed and was hanging on the wall of the manager's office. There it presumably remains to this day, since Bob never had the nerve to tell the truth and eventually went back to Ireland leaving the firm in their blissful ignorance.

So this practical joke is still undetonated, and with this book you are receiving, absolutely free of extra charge, a Sense of Power. One day you may find yourself in a Canadian office on the wall of which hangs a framed letter signed *M. Bissell.* You will then have in your hands the awesome responsibility of deciding whether or not to bring the dream world of that company crashing about its ears.

On a rather larger scale, Ireland has also had a forged giant. As I mentioned, the waters of Lough Neagh are supposed to have the property of turning things into stone; so that, for example, a piece of holly immersed in Lough Neagh is said to hone a razor sharp enough, in the local expression, "to shave a mouse asleep." In the 19th Century some enterprising showmen took advantage of this to announce that they had discovered in Lough Neagh the petrified body of the legendary Irish giant Finn McCoul, and produced a three ton sculpture made for them by an Italian artist so conscientious that he had even put six toes on the right foot, a sure indication of supernatural powers. They exhibited this with great profit throughout Northern Ireland, and then in Liverpool and Manchester, until one of the showmen fell out with the others over his share of the proceeds. He took out an injunction against them and the giant became the largest ward ever in chancery. However, the case was dropped and Finn McCoul ended up in the left luggage office at Worship Street Railroad Station in London, where he must have been a considerable embarrassment to the railroad company. Sixty-five years later he was still there, and the storage charges had accumulated to over two thousand dollars. Eventually the Luftwaffe solved the problem by bombing the railroad station and demolishing Finn McCoul, whose remains were used to fill the crater.

A more classic Irish hoax was that of the so-called Woman of Mungret, a place near Limerick, which is remembered from the days of the early Irish Church.

The scholars of the monastery there had been challenged to a contest in erudition, or as we would now say, a quiz, by the scholars of a neighboring monastery. They were conscious of their limitations, so they conceived the idea of disguising themselves as washerwomen and stationing themselves beside a bridge their opponents would cross on the way to the contest. When the visiting team appeared they started talking among themselves in Greek and Latin, which so astonished their hearers that they stopped and asked how mere washerwomen came to be so well educated. The "washerwomen" explained that they worked for Mungret monastery, where the scholars were so erudite one could acquire a classical education merely by overhearing their conversation. "If this is what their washerwomen are like what chance have we got against the monks themselves?" said the opponents in dismay, and they turned and went home. Which explains why the expression "as wise as a Mungret woman" is used in Limerick.

It also takes us back to the concept of deceit as a method of self-defense. Blarney might be said to be part of the Irish armory too. It originally meant evasiveness, deriving from the difficulty Queen Elizabeth had getting a straight answer from the Earl of Blarney when he didn't want to give one, but later meant the sort of flattery called soft soap by the English when they see through it. Among their hangers-on in Ireland it degenerated into a sort of whining servility now only found among the itinerant people called tinkers, but ordinarily it was and is a form of hospitality. Just as the Irishmen would give to a guest any physical comfort he could, he would also try to make him happy in other ways.

The tourist notices this today most obviously in the almost embarrassing trouble people will take to show him his way, or give other help. I have never known a country where people have undergone such agony of mind in deciding whether or not to tip. Another source of embarrassment is the notorious Irish habit of telling visitors that the distance to where they want to go is much less than it is. In remote areas this may be because they are still thinking in Irish miles, but more often it is simply because they feel that since you have to go there anyway you may as well start in good heart.

To my cost I have found that sometimes they will even prefer to give you doubtful directions rather than appear to be inhospitable by saying they don't know. I remember once I had to get in a hurry from Cork to Cobh to catch a boat for America, and a group of people standing in line for a bus told me the Monkstown ferry would get me there in half an hour. I believed them because I didn't know exactly where Cobh was. All I knew about it was that when Laurel and Hardy landed there for a tour of Europe in the evening of their lives, all the church bells played their cuckoo theme. It is a fine thing to know about any town, but a map would have been more helpful. It would have saved me a one hour bus trip to Monkstown and a voyage across part of the North Atlantic in a Force Nine gale in a rowing boat manned by two small boys.

However, I could forgive them anything for what they did for Stan and Ollie. I forget where I read about the church bells, but I have remembered it for years. Many people have memories like that of Ireland, for the country has a genius for saying and doing the right thing. In the courtesy without coldness and the service without servility the visitor receives in Ireland he will learn something of its history, for this tact and sensitivity is what one might expect from a man whose father was a servant but whose grandfather was a king.

When unpleasant things have to be done, they are done as pleasantly as possible. In one of Frank O'Connor's stories he tells of a policeman calling at a mountain farm to collect a fine imposed by the court for some small offense. Having climbed up the mountain the policeman greets the old man as if he just happened to be passing, asks after his relatives, is invited in for a glass of suspiciously pale whiskey, and stays for tea. As darkness falls he takes his leave and then pauses a few feet outside the door to ask, "I don't suppose you'd be thinking of paying that wee biteen of a fine they put on you a while back?" Notice that the policeman has allied himself firmly with the old man against "them" and implied that the paying of the fine would be a courtly and voluntary act, making it pleasanter for the old man to pay the fine if he can and less embarrassing for him if he cannot.

The same sort of thing is illustrated in the Dublin joke about an old woman coming back from the pub with a pot of porter concealed under her shawl. She stops to talk to a neighbor and in the interest of the conversation her grip on the pot slackens so that the porter drips onto the pavement. The neighbor notices this and knows quite well what it is, but is momentarily at a loss to know how to mention it without embarrassment. Finally she burst out, "Mrs. Murphy, you're losing your message."

In a way, you might say that Ireland's birthright is that pot of message.

14. The Pope's Green Isle

One day the vivacious wife of a minor politician called at Westminster with an invitation to dinner for Charles Stuart Parnell, the Uncrowned King of Ireland. As she leaned from her carriage a rose fell from her bodice. The usually austere Parnell picked it up and kissed it, and put it in his buttonhole. When he died in disgrace eleven years later the rose was found among his private papers with the name, Katharine O'Shea, and the date, 16th July 1880, and it was buried with him in his coffin. On top of the coffin was a huge wreath with the inscription MURDERED BY THE PRIESTS.

The indictment was significant, but unjust. To have expected the Church to support agrarian revolt in Ireland was to expect a sow's ear from a silk purse. The Church was concerned with the eternal soul of man, and only secondarily with his material difficulties during his brief sojourn in this world. Since the Church and its teachings were the means of the soul's salvation, it followed that no amount of human misery could justify disregard of its moral authority or diminution of its temporal power.

In Ireland it faced a problem rather like its present one in South America. It was in the nature of the situation that all effective movements to remedy the state of affairs in Ireland involved violence, and this the

Church could not approve. It did not condemn these movements because they were led by Protestants; it would be more true to say that they were led by Protestants because the Church condemned them. The clergy in Ireland supported the Protestant Parnell as long as his movement did not, in the words of Leo XIII, "cast aside obedience to lawful rulers."

However, Parnell's popularity soon began to alarm the Church and the apparently imminent prospect of home rule in Ireland was not viewed in the Vatican with any great enthusiasm. An independent Ireland led by a Protestant might not give the Church its rightful place, and the removal of nearly a hundred Irish members from the British Parliament would weaken Catholic influence on the affairs of the great British Empire. The opportunity to reassert the spiritual supremacy of the Church in Ireland seemed to have arrived in 1883, when an Irish newspaper started a fund to pay off the mortgage on the Parnell estate in County Wicklow. (Parnell had been allowing his tenants to live virtually rent-free and was by now himself very poor.) It was clearly wrong that the little money the average Irish Catholic had to spare should be diverted from the needs of the Church to the exigencies of a Protestant, and after some diplomatic prompting by the British Government the Vatican issued a rescript to the effect that it was the duty of the clergy to "curb the excited feelings of the multitude" with respect to Mr. Parnell.

The response was immediate and startling, but not quite the one the Church had expected. Irish contributions to the Church fell to the lowest level since the Famine period and the Parnell Fund, which had leveled off at less than forty thousand dollars, reached two hundred thousand dollars within a year. The cry throughout the country was, "Make Peter's Pence into Parnell Pounds." The English Prime Minister commented ruefully, "It is absurd to think that the Pope exercises any influence in Irish politics."

The Church tried again four years later. It was now concerned about boycotting, which was proving so cruelly effective a weapon against the grasping landlords and their agents. After sending an emissary to investigate the situation in Ireland the Vatican issued a circular:

In disputes between letters and holders of farms in Ireland, is it lawful to have recourse to . . . boycotting. . . . Their Eminences having long and maturely weighed the matter unanimously replied: In the negative.

Their Eminences went on to add that the reply had been approved and confirmed by the Holy Father, and directed the Irish bishops to admonish the people.

One would have thought that this instruction was reasonably clear for an ecclesiastical pronouncement, but the Vatican had underestimated the determination and ingenuity of the Irish Catholic. Within twenty-four hours an article in an influential Irish newspaper, obviously inspired if not actually written by a prominent theologian, offered some help in interpreting this "highly technical document." While of course one must look to the bishops for an authentic interpretation, the writer pointed out with great scholarship, the vital distinction is to be drawn between the authority of the Pope on questions of doctrine and his opinion on matters of fact. If the assumptions on which the Pope had based his pronouncement were not in accord with the realities of the situation, the doctrinal pronouncement itself was inapplicable.

It was clear to everyone that the Pope had indeed misunderstood the situation in Ireland, and with a sigh of relief the country carried on boycotting. The Irish Parliamentary Party passed a resolution to the effect that "Irish Catholics can recognize no right in the Holy See to interfere with the Irish people in the management of their political affairs." The Irish bishops, meeting after a series of mass demonstrations throughout the country in support of this attitude, issued a statement of a satisfactorily vague nature to the effect that while of course the Roman Pontiff had the right to speak with authority on faith and morals they were sure he did not intend to interfere with politics nor to injure the national movement.

Despairingly, the Pope himself issued an Encyclical condemning the "forced interpretations" of his decree, and reiterated that "the entire method of action whose employment We have forbidden is forbidden as altogether unlawful." Even this was cheerfully ignored by the Irish, apparently on the grounds that His Holiness was merely repeating himself and that this little misunderstanding had already been satisfactorily cleared up.

Twice bitten, the Church was shy of attacking Parnell when the newspapers began publishing the sordid details of his adulterous affair with Kitty O'Shea. Parnell was unanimously reelected leader of the Irish Parliamentary Party, and reassurances of support flooded in from all over Ireland. If any church did for Parnell, it was the Protestant one. The English Prime Minister believed that the English middle-class voter would not stand for Parnell, and offered the Irish the choice between him and Home Rule. As it happened they got neither for, torn between loyalty and expediency, the movement fell apart. Only then did the Church join in the attack on Parnell. It did not bring him down, far less kill him; the worst that could be said for it is that, finding a wounded enemy defenseless, it helped finish him off.

When Parnell died a year after the scandal, his sanity had already gone, he had made enemies of his friends, and he had been rejected by the Irish electorate. But nevertheless when the news of his death came through, shops and offices closed throughout Ireland. He had been a man who, in the Ulster phrase, did not have to stand up twice to cast a shadow. The death had been sudden and the funeral too soon for elaborate arrangements, and the priest had told the parishioners not to attend. But in Dublin 160,000 of them did, among them a young poet called Yeats.

Many people believed that the coffin was filled with stones, and that one day Parnell would come again: a traditional comfort not available to the people nowadays when they are liable to see their leaders murdered live on television. Nearly twenty years later some people still believed Parnell was leading the Boers against the English in South Africa. In fact some of his spirit lived on in the young Yeats, another Anglo-Irish Protestant, who had drawn his own conclusions from Parnell's life and death. The Gaelic revival that Yeats inspired, which was to lead eventually to the Easter Rebellion of 1916, was to bypass Catholic Ireland for its inspiration and hark back to the Celtic pre-Christian Ireland of mythology.

In effect, the era of Papal Ireland had lasted only a few centuries out of Ireland's long history. In the 9th Century an Irish monk was deploring the pilgrimages some of his colleagues were making to Rome in a well-known verse:

> *To go to Rome*
> *Is little profit, endless pain.*
> *The Master that you seek in Rome*
> *You find at home, or seek in vain;*

and the continued independence of the Irish Church three hundred years later was one of the main reasons which led the Pope to encourage the invasion of the country by England. England then forged the present bonds between the Roman Catholic Church and the Irish people by persecuting both with equal severity when she herself turned Protestant in the 16th Century.

Those bonds are still strong, and the Roman Catholic hierarchy still has a powerful influence in the Republic of Ireland—though never so powerful, perhaps, as has been believed by the Protestants in the North, who tend to think of the Church as a monolithic menace. The controversy there about the Pope's latest Encyclical, if it does nothing else, may have shown the North that Southern Catholicism is about as monolithic as the beach at Bray, if no less permanent.

The controversy itself took much the same form as it did elsewhere in the world, except perhaps that the pro-Papal forces were quicker off the mark. Within twenty-four hours they were assuring the Pope that all Ireland was behind him, without taking the precaution to call the roll. An Irish doctor who volunteered the support of his profession was disowned in an article in the *Irish Medical Times*, which described the Encyclical as a bombshell which had thrown the entire Catholic community into confusion, and its doctrine to be medically unsound and untenable. A later poll confirmed that the great majority of the Irish medical profession was behind that view. A prominent Catholic layman who had leaped onto the nonexistent bandwagon was brought to earth and jumped on for declaring that God had spoken through the Pope. A particularly withering letter in the *Irish Times* congratulated him for correcting the oversight the Pope had made in not claiming this himself: obviously he should have awaited the Encyclical to be issued by this infallible Irish primate, who would perhaps "at some future time let us know how God is getting on, and convey our regards to Him."

The views of doctors were explained in more detail in a BBC television program recorded in Dublin. The doctor at a child welfare clinic in a working class suburb said he would continue to prescribe the Pill for mothers whose health would be endangered by further childbirth. He was obviously not only a great and kindly man, but he had a fine command of language: "This Encyclical is asking me to commit murder, cold-blooded murder. I am a doctor and I will not do it. I would like the Pope to come to my clinic and see these little children with their eyes lit up in love for their mother, and they with nothing else in the whole world, and then tell me I should take their mother away from them. None of us can know what these great and good women have already been through. I know when I am in the presence of sanctity, and I tell you these women are saints. They say I am to murder these saints and I say I won't. These theologians flapping their pieces of paper and saying the Irish people agree with the Pope are only confusing the poor man further." This was the doctor who went on to compare the Irish love of religion with their addiction to horse-racing.

The interviews with the saints themselves were distinguished by their disarming honesty. The interviewer unguardedly asked one what people would do if the Pill were withheld; he passed hastily on before she explained exactly what she meant by taking the kettle off before it boiled. The majority opinion seemed to be that families, husbands and their own health took the first three places, with the Pope coughing in the stable. As for middle-class women, a gynaecologist in private practice said that of two hundred of his patients who were using the Pill as a contraceptive, only one had changed her mind as a result of the Encyclical.

Nobody seems to know how many Irish women are on the Pill. One estimate was as low as eighteen thousand, but the editor of a provincial newspaper told me that in his opinion most young married women were using it; if their own doctor wouldn't prescribe it they went to one who would. In Belfast, a Catholic girl complained to me that the Pill was hindering her housework. It used to be that all the young married women went through confession like an assembly line: now she has to wait while each spends up to twenty minutes in the confessional, most of them in heated argument.

It is the public aspect of this argument which is the most interesting development in Ireland, for while criticism of the Church among the people has always been common enough, it has usually been of the "Mind you I've said nothing" variety. But for weeks in August, 1968, Irish newspapers were filled with controversy, including vast numbers of letters—indignant, delighted, bitter, complacent, poignant and triumphant—from ordinary people who had never written to a newspaper before. The doctrines and authority of the Church were now being openly called to question in the established organs of public opinion, a ventilation which must be healthy for relations between the Church and the people.

It is hard to assess what the majority opinion is, because people do not always do what they say; and in Ireland especially they tend to say what their questioner wants to hear. This tendency was not corrected by a question in a public opinion poll conducted by a pro-clerical Irish newspaper which, barely audible above the spinning noises coming from the graves of the founders of psephology, asked: "Do you not agree that the Pope's prohibition of the Pill should be accepted by Irish Catholics?" Nevertheless, the newspaper eventually admitted that people were making their opinions clear and that "the majority view was in line with that of the doctors."

As for the eventual outcome, it is probably not true that the Encyclical is already as dead as the dodo, as *The Economist* thinks, but my own guess is that most people in Ireland will continue to do as they themselves think right, justifying themselves by one ingenious line of reasoning or another. Like the Irish monk who, under a vow to keep silent unless speech was necessary to help others, found a mouse in his soup. After a moment's thought he pointed to his neighbor's plate and complained, "My friend has no mouse in his soup."

15. Love in a Damp Climate

"In respect of the recurrent emergence of the theme of sex in his characters," said the New York judge who raised the ban on James Joyce's *Ulysses*, "it must always be remembered that his locale was Celtic and his season spring." It might also have been remembered that Joyce's two principal characters were a Jew of Hungarian descent and a girl from Gibraltar. Joyce knew the Dublin of 1904 far too well to represent it as a hotbed of Celtic sensuality. The brothels of its Nighttown were, as he might have put it, a buy-product of the Brutish garrison, and were soon to become a whory legend. The minute the English soldiers were out of them the Legion of Mary had moved in, converting them into decent Christian slums.

However, the image of the passionate Irishman, a brothel of a bhoy and a multiplier of his species, was not seriously dented until the publication a dozen or so years ago of O'Brien's *The Vanishing Irish*. This alarming book pointed out that the number of Irish marriages was so few and the happy couples so old, that unless the Irish got on the ball they would all be extinct in less than a hundred years. Various culprits were arraigned, and discharged with stains on their characters. They included the Government, the Catholic Church, and, most worrying of all, the sexual inadequacy of the Irish male.

"Soap and education are not as sudden as a massacre," said Mark Twain, "but they are more deadly in the long run." It is true that when people are able to stop living like animals they cease to breed like animals, and to that extent Mark Twain was right. But since his time it has turned out to the surprise of all the experts that people like children and have them when they can afford to provide for them, so that the birth rate rises again. It may be that the Government in Ireland has done enough to bring the people out of the rabbit stage, but then, by collaborating with the Church in prohibiting contraception, has discouraged the responsible procreation of children which has been found to accompany prosperity in other countries. Young people nowadays do not contemplate with eagerness a married life consisting entirely of pregnancy and poverty, abstinence or worry.

Apart from that it seems the Government must be absolved, because the Irish in America are not all that keen on marriage either. Some people point out that all the immigrants brought with them was their clergy, and put all the blame on the puritan outlook of the Irish Church. It is true that some of the clergy in Ireland have behaved peculiarly at times. Priests have enforced sexual segregation in cinemas, prohibited dances, smashed crossroads dancing boards, spied on and denounced courting couples, fulminated from the pulpit against "company keeping" and have even been known to denounce Woman as the "unclean vessel." But this perverted thinking is not Catholic doctrine and these minds are not only sick but heretical, a relic of the Jansenist movement, with which Irish Catholicism was tainted by refugee priests from the French Revolution.

Again, some blame the understandable desire of many Irish familes to have a son in the priesthood, if only as a steady job with good prospects, both in this world and the next. They say it has led to a widespread feeling that married people are second-class Catholics. But in the Church itself there is great concern about the low marriage rate, and *The Vanishing Irish* was full of constructive suggestions for action by other people. Some advocated marriage and family allowances, others taxes on bachelors and spinsters; the *Ave Maria* suggested that bachelors be put in prison until they promised to find a mate; Father Noonon advocated inheritance on marriage, a sort of economic euthanasia for old people; Father Hayes advocated stimulating the Irish rural economy, pointing out that young men were being drawn to England by higher wages there "and perhaps a feeling of a free leg, too." (I hope I know what he means.) But the most dramatic suggestion came from an anonymous priest who advocated the importation into Ireland of five thousand virile young Italians or Poles to "set an example."

What all these seem to have in common is the assumption that the young Irishman has to be bribed or coerced or shamed into performing a function for which young men elsewhere find the natural inducements provided by young ladies quite sufficient. It is clear that these natural inducements are offered by the Irish colleen too, judging by the way her feet are hardly allowed to touch the ground between the gangplank of the boat to England and the nearest Registry Office, and the blame is allowed to fall unfairly and squarely on the Irish male. He is, it is said, lazy, selfish and mean; a gawky lover and an inconsiderate husband; interested only in drink, gambling and argument; without enough sex, as Arrland Ussher put it, to perpetuate his own cantankerous species. If this is what is wrong, I wonder why no one has suggested replacing the Censorship Board by one charged with the dissemination of pornography.

I know of at least one girl in Ireland who would hardly agree with that diagnosis. She is the American student in a recent court case who within a few hours of her arrival in the country had been raped by no less than three men. They were not acting as a gang, but the mere fact that there were more than two of them constituted them an "unlawful assembly" within the meaning of a statute designed to deal with political outrages, and she became entitled to a large sum in compensation from the Government. You'll understand that the Tourist Board cannot guarantee this attraction, and that I am not advancing it as evidence of anything except the danger of generalizing from individual experiences. From this one might deduce that Irish men are all sex-mad and Irish girls so unattractive that in desperation the Government is subsidizing mass rape.

Again, the fact that some Irish girls seem to prefer English boys is sometimes advanced as evidence of the sexual inadequacy of the young Irish male. But I talked to one of these girls, a pretty receptionist, and asked her just why she preferred to go out with English boys. She said they "knew how to treat a girl," they were "more tactful," they were prepared to "regard women as friends," whereas Irish boys were only after "the one thing." Translating this into masculine terms I surmise it means that she went out with boys she didn't go for, and when they'd spent their money on her as a girl, she switched her role to that of platonic friend. Her objection to Irish boys was apparently not that they were undersexed, but that they objected to her obtaining money by false pretenses.

She was quite right, however, to some extent, in that Irishmen are not romantic in the modern sense of the word. Even their poets tend to be very practical people. Brendan Behan told a very illuminating story about W. B. Yeats, the greatest and most mystical of all. A friend of his called Smyllie had the privilege of telephoning the great poet to tell him he had won the Nobel Prize, which he was doing with great pride and solemnity when Yeats interrupted: "For Jesus' sake, Smyllie, pull yourself together. How much?"

So while there is plenty of love in Irish poetry, there is not much romance. A very typical folk song is "The Maid of the Sweet Brown Knowe," which tells of a girl who lives on a hill overlooking the farm of her suitor. He points out its richness as an inducement to marriage, but she demurs on the grounds that he is known to visit the village inn and to "rap and to call and to pay for all, and go home at the break of day." The song ends with his withering reply:

> If I rap and I call and I pay for all, the money is all
> my own.
> I'll never spend your fortune, for I hear that you've
> got none.
> You thought you had my poor heart broken talking to
> me now,
> But I'll leave you where I found you, at the foot of the
> sweet brown knowe.

In defense of this unchivalrous farewell reported by Anon., 18th Century, it is only fair to point out that the whole idea of romantic love is quite a recent innovation, and impinged on the people of Ireland only about the same time as the steam engine, along with compulsory education in English. It had originated among the mediaeval aristocracy, who could afford the fun of fighting and the luxury of languishing over idealized womanhood. Death from unrequited love has never ranked high in Irish mortality statistics, and the conventions of chivalry were foreign to Irish thought. Chivalry was to a large extent founded on the tacit assumption that women had no rights of their own, or at least no power to enforce them, and resembled to some extent the code of conduct followed by humane slave owners. Whereas in Irish society women had very firm and definite rights, in some respects greater than those of men. They were given special protection against violence, the fines for assault on them being double those for attacking men. Even to pull a woman's hair brought a fine equivalent to something like three hundred dollars. A wife's consent was necessary before her husband could make a contract. She could divorce him for cruelty or neglect; for sterility, impotence, homosexuality or becoming a priest; for mental cruelty (making her an object of mockery or betraying the secrets of the marriage bed); even for becoming too fat. And having done so she could remarry without stigma or difficulty. This system of law continued for many hundreds of years after the introduction of Christianity, being tolerated by the Irish Church until Rome asserted her authority. "It cannot be doubted," says the German scholar August Knock, "that the cultural progress implied in the manifest respect for the individual personality of the wife in Irish marriage law, in contrast with the base position of women in earlier periods or among other peoples, constitutes a shining landmark in this early period of western history."

So for most of Ireland's history love between man and woman was a simple and direct cleaving together of two free and equal individuals holding each other in mutual respect. But in the latter half of the 19th Century the situation had become considerably more complicated. Women had now only the paltry rights accorded them by English law, but still were regarded as equals in Irish social relationships. On this dual standard was now superimposed a concept of chivalry imported from a society where women had never had any rights. Then, with the increased Irish ownership of land after Parnell, the course of true love was increasingly thwarted by the complications of the rural economy, every marriage tending to involve a complex reallocation of land. And finally the priest was preaching on alternate Sundays God's commandment to replenish the earth and his own abhorrence of the only method yet discovered for accomplishing this end. It hardly seems surprising that the Irish youth, enjoined simultaneously to regard women as chattels, partners, matriarchs, goddesses and unclean vessels, gets a little confused at times; and, noting the closure of the escape hatches of birth control and divorce, thinks long before tying himself for life to one of these composite creatures.

However, there is evidence that his heart is still in the right place under the cloak of respectability, and the rest of his organs also. The amorousness of the Irish, which foreigners used constantly to remark on, survives

in bawdy folksong, and the best of their modern literature, handily signposted for discerning readers by the
former Censorship Board, shows a continuing healthy
interest in sex.

Even the rituals of paganism have shown a remarkable vitality. In pre-Christian times there was a great
festival at Telltown (Taillteann), County Meath, on the
first weekend in August (later August Bank Holiday)
to commemorate the wedding of Lug, the Sun God,
with Erin, the incarnation of Ireland. Even in quite modern times young people would go there for trial marriages, and living in sin is still known in some parts of
Ireland as a Telltown Marriage. The trial marriage could
be dissolved after one year by the pair returning to Telltown, standing back to back, and walking away from
each other. No doubt one day the enterprising Tourist
Board will see the potentialities in this. Again, Schrier,
in *Ireland and the American Emigration*, reports that
it was the custom of young men who had to leave their
girl friends behind in Ireland to take with them a lock
of their pubic hair as a love charm—a practice it is hard
to reconcile with the accepted chastely romantic picture
of Irish courtship.

Fortunately for the image of the Rose of Tralee, this
touching custom is said to have been peculiar to Ulster,
and will no doubt be regarded by Catholic puritans as
further evidence for their theory that Ulster people are
sex-mad materialists. The main argument for what
might be called the Sex County Theory has been that
Northern Ireland has the highest illegitimate birth rate
in the British Isles, and the Republic of Ireland the
lowest. However, when one considers that a girl finding herself pregnant in the Republic of Ireland has only

to take the train to Northern Ireland or the ferry to England to secure for herself anonymity, free hospitalization and the services of eager adoption societies, the remarkable feature of the statistics is that any illegitimate births are recorded in the Republic at all. One doubts if the theory of the impregnable colleen would last long if babies, like other imported manmade products, were stamped on the bottom with the country of origin.

Even the statistics about the legitimate Irish birth rate are misinterpreted. It is certainly true that a small number of Irishmen are either seriously undersexed, or more likely have been daunted into drowning their natural instincts in drink or sublimating them in religion, and are not procreating at all. But it is also true that if emigration were to fall the Irish birth rate would be more than adequate to maintain the population. It seems to follow then that the majority of Irishmen are doing a good job under tremendous difficulties. To say the birth rate statistics prove the average Irishman has a low sex drive is as misleading as to ignore the difference between men and women and to announce to the world the startling statistical discovery that the average human being in Ireland has only one testicle. Indeed Catholic puritanism itself, evinced by such past aberrations as the Censorship Board, is evidence of a neurotic preoccupation with sex. It is high time, Gogarty said, that the people of this country found some other way of loving God, than by hating women. Like so many of the faults of modern Ireland its prevalence is attributable to the Famine.

Until the Famine the population of Ireland had been increasing and since the Famine it has been falling, and there is no need to look for the reason anywhere but in the Famine itself. First, even in merely physical terms, it was proportionately the worst disaster ever to befall a people in the whole history of the world. Second, it struck them through the land of Ireland itself, which was as if the motherland had poisoned her children, as if the Nazi gas chambers had been in Israel. Third, it left no hope: the Famine was the final blow in a program of racial destruction, from which the only escape was flight from the accursed country. Fourth, death was lingering and degrading. Fifth, it had been avoidable by human effort, so was not an act of God. Sixth, it took the best of the race: the proud, the generous, those of high metabolism. And seventh, it was not localized and complete like an earthquake; it left the memories of mothers who had watched their babies die and of children crying beside the emaciated bodies of their parents.

These memories remained, and are now enshrined in the behavior patterns of aging Irish bachelors and their possessive mothers. Security is, they feel, to be found only in religion, and fulfillment only in the next life. Human nature is naturally depraved, and cannot be saved by character and effort, only by the grace of God. All human instincts and desires are to be distrusted and denied. The greatest snare is sex, leading as it does to either mortal sin or the worldly institution of marriage, a resort for those incapable of celibacy and permitted only for the unpleasant duty of procreation. Children are hostages to fortune and their arrival a punishment for self-indulgence. As if in some cosmic project of aversion therapy these people had been turned off life by the traumatic shock of the Famine, to an outlook almost identical with that of the Jansenist heresy. As Martin Ross put it, ice water from the snows of the Famine still shivers in the veins of Ireland.

It may be that this phase is part of a process of racial self-purification, necessary to the regeneration of Ireland. Or that the country has been left encumbered with a proportion of low-drive, slave mentalities, and that the Jansenist philosophy they find so attractive is a form of self-sterilization which is painlessly removing them from the scene. Even that the obstacles placed in the way of marriage in the Republic of Ireland are for a time desirable as a way of insuring that only the virile and independently minded perpetuate themselves. Presumably it is the fear that there may not be enough of them left in Ireland that prompted that priest to suggest the importation of five thousand studs from Poland.

There would be a geat deal to be said for the importation of some new genes, since Ireland has had an adverse trade balance in this commodity for far too long. The children of Poles would make as good Irishmen as have the descendants of the English, Normans and Danes, or for that matter of the Celts that came from Egypt by way of Spain. But otherwise I doubt if they will be needed. Even priests do not know all that goes on in Ireland, as I found when I asked my wife why she giggled at the BBC program *Come Dancing*. She spent several perilous holidays as a teenager in Tipperary and found that country *ceilidhes* are not always the decorous affairs they are supposed to be. Her feeling was that Irishmen will surmount their obstacles without the aid of Poles.

16. The Rats that Ate the Railroad

Subjectively, Ireland is bigger than the United States. Whatever geographers may say, the effective size of a country is measured in the time it takes to get from one end of it to the other, and in those terms Cork is further from Belfast than Los Angeles is from New York. However desperate your urgency, you simply cannot get from one of these provincial capitals to the other in less than six hours, and you can only manage that if you are able to use both the express train services that run between them and Dublin. The journey across the country in the diagonally opposite direction is more dauntingly complex than the one from Seattle to Miami, and would take more than a day by any combination of public transport. Ireland has no internal air services because the population is too small, too dispersed and not rich enough to support them—handicaps which have plagued all modern forms of transport in the country.

In 1787 there were 257 private sedan chairs in Dublin, a statement I offer for the delectation of connoisseurs of utterly useless information. However, it is illuminating to know that they were still in use as late as 1840, as evidenced by a popular joke of that period which will now be told for probably the last time. A countryman visiting Dublin expressed wonderment at the sedan chairs and his Dublin friends offered him a trip in one of them, from which they had first removed the floor. After trotting him up and down several dirty streets they asked him what he thought of this mode of travel. "Well," he said, "only for the honor and glory of the thing, it was mighty like walking." In fact, transport was unknown to most of the population: they walked where they wanted to go. Every winter farm laborers walked from Connaught to Dublin to find work, a distance of well over two hundred miles. By contrast, another connoisseur of useless information who is also a light railroad enthusiast told me that at one time early in this century it was possible to travel all the way from New York to Chicago in three days using only urban trolley car systems.

The first and probably the only man to have run a really successful transport undertaking in Ireland was an Italian called Bianconi, who introduced the first "long car" stage coach. Even he had some difficulty at first persuading the natives to make use of his new-fangled contraption, until he hit on the bright idea of buying another coach under another name and racing against it. The excitement of a break-neck race was more appealing to the Irish than the mere saving of time, but having experienced both, the middle classes gleefully accepted the new tempo of life and soon a profitable Bianconi service covered the whole country: demonstrating that only the brave deserve the fare.

When the railways came Bianconi bought shares, and, with the sound commercial instinct which had marked his entire career, died while they were still rising in value. The promoters who followed him suffered from the disadvantage that many of their potential passengers were now clambering onto trolley cars in America, and the Irish railway bandwagon ground to a shuddering halt.

It was exciting while it lasted, particularly in the narrow gauge county of the West. The West Clare Railroad, the one that used to carry Kate O'Brien to Kilkee, had started off with the distinction of being one of the few railroads to have one of its locomotives sunk. During trials it fell off the track into a bog and was never seen again. The railroad itself died only a few years ago, with a song in its heart. In its heyday it had carried many stage personalities to entertain the holiday crowds at Kilkee, and one of them was the comedian and song-writer Percy French, who wrote "The Mountains of Mourne" and other stage Irish songs. He wrote one about the West Clare Railroad, called "Are Ye Right There, Michael," which alleged that among other unbusinesslike practices the company required its passengers to get out and gather fuel. Highly indignant, the company sued him for libel. Unfortunately for them their witnesses did not turn up for the hearing in time, the train having been delayed. Rather than proffer this ignominious explanation, the company hastily settled out of court.

Even more unfortunate was another company in Galway, which lost its whole railroad overnight. Its line was to run from Shannon Harbor to Portumna, but had reached only halfway when the money ran out. For some years the track and stations and equipment lay there untouched, and then a vagrant was arrested by the police for stealing a lantern. The local population showed a peculiar interest in the case. At the trial nobody appeared on behalf of the company to prove ownership of the lantern, possibly because it owed money in the district. Next morning the entire railroad had vanished off the face of the earth, and to this day tactless visitors are prone to remark on the unusual solidity of the farm outbuildings and fences in the area.

Which reminds me of a man in Belfast who worked for the city trolley car company and was not averse to bringing home for domestic use any item of equipment or furniture for which his employers did not seem to have any immediate use. It was said of him locally that if you were to ring a bell in the street his whole house would move off.

An even more shattering misfortune happened to a canal company. Canals were a great way to travel in those days, in luxurious barges with dining accommodation, and one thriving company decided to expand its operations into the limestone region north of Clare. They hewed the new canal out of the rock and a beautiful job it was, all clean and neat for the opening ceremony. After much speech-making and mutual congratulation the water was let in, foamed along the canal for a few yards, and disappeared from view. No doubt it reappeared again somewhere else after traversing some subterranean channel, but it left the canal as high and dry as the company.

But possibly the most poignant of all was the fate of the Atmospheric Railway, invented in 1840 by Samual Clegg and Joseph Sands. Irish adaptation to the Industrial Revolution tended to be erratic, since machines do not respond readily to eloquence, nor are they easily moved by flattery; so with some exceptions, like the pneumatic tire invented by John Dunlop of Belfast, contributions of the native Irish tended to be impractical, or as they would prefer to put it, in advance of their time. So certainly it was with the Atmospheric Railway.

The motive power for this ingenious contrivance was supplied by two pumps, one at each end of a long metal tube about fifteen inches in diameter, running the whole length of the track between the rails. A pump at one terminus sucked air out of the tube, the other one at the other terminus pumped air in, and between them they propelled along the tube a piston to which the train was attached. To permit the coupling between the train and the piston, a slot ran the whole length of the tube, sealed with strips of metal and heavily waxed leather rather like a zip fastener. On the underside of the train there was fixed a fork to prize the zip open; immediately after that the iron arm by which the train was coupled to the piston; immediately after that rollers for closing the tube up again; and finally, just to make sure, a little coal furnace to melt the wax and insure an airtight seal.

The model worked beautifully and everyone was tremendously impressed. Speeds of up to eighty miles per hour were said to be theoretically possible. The great railway engineer Brunel recommended this new type of railroad for the line between Croydon and London. The English Board of Trade, more cautious but still enthusiastic, gave twenty-five thousand pounds for the construction of a track between Kingston and Dalkey, near Dublin. This was duly built, and was opened on March 29th, 1844.

It was "a triumphant success," climbing the one and three-quarters miles of sharp curves and steep hills up to Dalkey in three and one-half minutes and coasting back to Kingston in four minutes by gravity. Dr. Kane, in his *Industrial Resources of Ireland*, published in 1845, acclaimed it as a "remarkable mechanism of locomotion. The more intimate connection with the line by the pipe and piston gives steadiness to the atmospheric train, enabling it to traverse curves too steep for the safe passage of an ordinary train. Besides that, the absence of the locomotive, from which in most cases of accident the injury is sustained, presents an additional source of safety." Two hardheaded Belfast businessmen floated a company for the construction of a similar line from Belfast to Holywood, County Down.

Fortunately for them, they took a close look at the maintenance problems of the Kingstown-Dalkey line before actually spending any money of their own. There was already visible a cloud no bigger than a man's hand. No doubt to us the Atmospheric Railway seems a harebrained scheme, but it did work, and I wonder how many of us sophisticates could have anticipated that rats would take a fancy to the wax that sealed the tube. The Belfast businessmen guessed what was going to happen and hastily sold out to the Belfast and County Down Railway Company. Sure enough, word got around among the rat population that there was a one and three-quarter mile long banqueting table spread with food all the way from Kingstown to Dalkey, and soon the leather flaps were being gnawed away faster than they could be replaced. The railroad profits were being eaten up, closely followed by the railway itself, and now all that is left of it is a street sign in Dalkey reading mysteriously *Atmospheric Road*.

It is tempting to think that if in those days synthetic materials had been available the Atmospheric Railway might have become as important as steam, but the speculation is impractical because all the components of a technology march together. That was not the time for plastics and prosperity, but for rats and disaster.

Or was it. Only a few miles from the rapacious rats an Irishman had just accomplished what a modern astronomer refers to as a scientific miracle. Completely unaided he had built the largest telescope in the world and was making discoveries fundamental to modern astrophysics.

This contemporary Mount Palomar was at Birr Castle, County Offaly, and was the work of the Earl of Rosse. Hitherto the largest telescope in the world had been the forty-nine inch reflector made by the great Sir William Herschel in England. The Earl of Rosse determined to make one of seventy-two inches. In those days it was not possible to use glass for such a huge mirror, so the Earl cast one of metal, in a specially designed forge. It was nearly six inches thick, weighed four tons and took four months to cool down. Then it had to be ground down and polished, and this the Earl did single-handed. Simultaneously he supervised the construction of the tube in which it was to be mounted, fifty-four feet long and so wide that a man could walk through it carrying an open umbrella. We know this because in fact the local dean did just that at the opening ceremony.

Photographs could not be taken through the telescope, but the Earl's drawings of what he saw excited astronomers: he had discovered the spiral nebulae, a vital clue to the nature of the universe. Scientists came to Birr from all over the world. The telescope remained the largest in the world until near the end of the century, and was still in use until 1908, having been used among other things to measure the heat radiated by the surface of the moon. The great metal mirror is now in the Science Museum in South Kensington, London, but the rest of the telescope and the massive walls that support it can still be seen in the grounds of Birr Castle, a memorial to the fact that Irishmen can sometimes make their impractical dreams come true.

17. The Shamrock and the Rose

"The lovely and the lonely bride," was how one Englishman thought of Ireland, "which we have wedded but have never won." Nearly a quarter of a century after the divorce had been made absolute, John Bull and Kathleen ni Houlihan were still exchanging recriminations. In May, 1945, Winston Churchill, on the end of the War in Europe, thundered over the BBC:

> *Owing to the action of Mr. de Valera, so much at variance with the temperament and instinct of Southern Irishmen who hastened to the battlefield to prove their ancient valour, the approaches which the Southern Irish ports and airfields could so easily have guarded were closed by the hostile aircraft and U-boats. This was indeed a deadly moment in our life, and if it had not been for the loyalty and friendship of Northern Ireland, we should have been forced to come to close quarters with Mr. de Valera, or perish forever from the earth.*

From Mr. de Valera's reply, delivered over Radio

Eireann four days later, it was only too obvious that the parties were as far from understanding one another as ever.

> *Mr. Churchill is proud of Britain's stand alone, after France had fallen and before America had entered the war. Could he not find in his heart the generosity to acknowledge that there is a small nation that stood alone, not for a year or two, but for several hundred years, against aggression; that endured spoilation, famines, massacres in endless succession; that was clubbed many times into insensibility but each time, on returning to consciousness, took up the fight anew; a small nation that could never be got to accept defeat and has never surrendered her soul?*

On each side of the Irish Sea an entire population applauded its leader, confident that the case he had made was unanswerable; while in Northern Ireland the child of the broken marriage glowed with pride and new maturity, having saved both its parents from the worst consequences of their folly.

The rest of the world found itself rather in the position of a spectator at a divorce court who has just heard two honest and well-intentioned people give entirely contradictory evidence. In the contested action *Bull v. ni Houlihan* the situation was further complicated by the fact that the erring husband seemed to be suffering from amnesia.

The English remember vaguely that there was some bother with the Irish a long time ago, but cannot understand why they keep on harping about it. When de Valera came to London for peace talks during the

Troubles, the English prime minister was asked how they had got on the first day. "I suppose we're making progress," he replied ruefully; "we've got as far as Cromwell." The only solution to the Irish problem, another Englishman once suggested in desperation, was to make the teaching of Irish history compulsory in England and ban it altogether in Ireland.

When an Englishman does learn something of the history of Ireland, it is apt to upset him dreadfully. It made the sophisticated Thackeray almost incoherent. "It is a frightful document against ourselves—one of the most melancholy stories in the whole world of insolence, rapine, brutal endless persecution. . . . There is no crime ever invented by the eastern or western barbarians, no torture of Roman persecutors or Spanish inquisitors, no tyranny of Nero or Alva but can be matched in the history of the English in Ireland."

But even the history of the English in Ireland is not quite the same as Irish history. I remember that as a schoolboy I used to think of the past as divided neatly into two parts: there was politics, which was controversial and to be found in newspapers; and there was history, which was dead politics with all the bones of contention hygienically removed by historians and neatly canned in books. But you only have to read two books to find that this is not so at all, and that the whole of history is still in dispute, down to the smallest question of fact.

Take for example the peculiar affair of Queen Victoria and the Battersea Dogs Home. It is widely believed in Ireland that Queen Victoria contributed only five pounds to famine relief in Ireland, and that she simultaneously contributed the same amount to Battersea Dogs Home to show what she thought of the Irish. English historians point out how unjust this accusation is since in fact the Queen headed the list of subscribers for the Irish with two thousand pounds out of her own pocket. The simpleminded Irish may have been confused by the fact that in the same year the British Parliament voted a hundred thousand pounds for Irish famine relief and two hundred thousand pounds for a scheme to beautify Battersea Park. (A sum, Leonard Wibberley commented dryly, which anyone who has seen Battersea Park must admit to have been inadequate.) The Irish historians concede that Queen Victoria did in fact contribute two thousand pounds, but point out that the sultan of Turkey was going to contribute ten thousand pounds until he was asked not to, for the look of the thing. Unless the English historians have any further comeback, one is left wondering if maybe the simpleminded Irish were not right all along about the Queen's attitude.

The same confusion exists even about the Famine itself, which as the most important event in Irish history we would think would have had all its circumstances clearly established. But the English have always tended to regard it as a natural disaster, whereas the Irish have thought of it as the Starvation, an act of genocide. In the course of it coroners' juries in Ireland repeatedly brought in verdicts of willful murder against the British prime minister, primarily on the grounds that enough food to keep the Irish alive was being taken out of the country under armed guard. It is certainly true that people nowadays would agree that the British prime minister might well have been brought to trial and convicted at least of manslaughter, but by the standards of his time he was acting quite correctly. The food was taken out with the idea that the money received for it could be used by the Irish to buy cheaper food; the demand would attract the supply in accordance with the sacred principles of free enterprise. It would have worked too, only for the unfortunate fact that the capitalist system did not happen to exist over most of Ireland. Currency notes were so unfamiliar that they were regarded as a sort of non-negotiable security and frequently pawned, and coins were stored away to pay the rent, without which the family would be evicted. And in this subsistence economy there were no merchants to import the food in the first place. Even when it became clear that the free enterprise system was not working it was still regarded as positively immoral to give away food for nothing, so the enfeebled survivors were set to earn it by digging useless ditches and roads to nowhere.

But uninformed public opinion was taking the peculiar attitude that the best thing to do with a starving child was to feed it, and the ordinary unsophisticated English people, in their lamentable ignorance of economic theory, were naïvely contributing vast sums to famine relief. Worse still, the charitable organizations were recklessly dishing out food to just any old starving child, without making the proper inquiries, such as whether it would have been starving in an ordinary winter anyway, or whether its father was really quite well-off except for being destitute. So the government took over and put the system on a proper footing by providing that nobody should get free food who had more than a quarter of an acre of land. Of course this meant that farmers had to sell their land for a bowl of soup, much to the delight of the English landowners, who were keen to

replace people with more profitable cattle, but nothing
. . . well, hardly anything, was further from the minds
of the government itself. It was merely the sort of
situation described by Clemenceau so unfairly in his remark that he didn't object to the English having an ace
up their sleeve, just to their belief that God put it there.

Unfortunately, the potato crop kept failing monoto-
nously every year and the Irish Famine became a bit of a
bore. "It is possible to have heard the tale of sorrow too
often," said the *London Times*. Worse still, a desperado
called O'Brien was urging the ungrateful Irish to revolt. They were so enfeebled that the great revolt a-
mounted to the seige of a few policemen in a cottage,
none of them being even injured, but O'Brien's language had so alarmed the English they convinced themselves that any more charitable donations would be
used to buy arms. A bore, a nuisance and now a menace,
the Irish people were left to die or emigrate. The government decided that the problem must be dealt with by the
"operation of natural causes" and even the Quakers gave
up in despair. An English economist feared that the
third year of the Famine, 1848, would not kill more
than a million people, which "would scarcely be enough
to do much good," but later the *London Times* viewed
with satisfaction the Final Solution to the Irish problem:
"This island of one hundred and sixty harbours, with its
fertile soil, with its noble rivers and beautiful lakes,
with fertile mines and riches of every kind, is being
cleared quietly for the interest and luxury of humanity."

(In the article about Ireland in an English encyclopedia for children, these events are neatly summarized as
follows: "The British government tried to help the
Irish, but they could not do anything about the blight,

and after it the Irish were more bitter against the English than before.")

The English have always loved Ireland, and felt that all it needed for perfection was the removal of the Irish. As Lord Salisbury said, "The instinctive feeling of an Englishman is to wish to get rid of an Irishman." Or, as the gardening books put it, the rose does not like to share its bed with other plants.

Part of the reason was the fear of becoming Irish themselves, and they felt towards those of their countrymen who had done so something of the uncomprehending horror caterpillars must feel for butterflies. The Elizabethan poet Spenser, whose poetry was full of love for Ireland and his prose of suggestions for starving the Irish out of existence, expressed this fascinated repugnance in an imaginary dialogue:

Eudoxus: *Are not they that once were English, English still?*

Iraenus: *No, for some of them are degenerated and growne almost more Irish, yea, and more malitious to the English than the Irish themselves.*

Eudoxus: *Is it possible that an Englishman, brought up in such sweet civilie as England affords, should find such a liking in that barbarous rudeness that he should forget his own nature and forgoe his own nation? How may this be?*

Iraenus: *So much can liberty and ill examples do . . . for they are more stubborne and disobedient to the law and government than the Irish be.*

Eudoxus: *Lord, how quickly doth that country alter one's nature!*

(Naturally the situation looked somewhat different from the Irish point of view. A contemporary Irish writer expressed his pleasure that "these princely English lords had given up their foreignness for a pure mind, their surliness for good manners, their stubbornness for sweet mildness, and their perverseness for hospitality.")

Efforts to suppress the Irish language, culture, customs, habits, dress and even their way of riding horses having failed, the only solution was to "exterminate and exile the country people of the Irishry." That any of them survived was due to the wise statesmanship of the Earl of Essex, who pointed out to Queen Elizabeth that it would be just as effective to deprive them of their land. "The force which shall bring about the one shall do the other without any show that such a thing is meant."

It was unusual for English statesmen to be so concerned about public opinion, since they were usually able to conceal their activities in Ireland from the rest of the world. (And even at one time from the Irish themselves. A history of Ireland for Irish schools used in 1910 describes the program of extermination and exile thus: "The natives dwelling on the rich tracts were migrated to the poor portion.") Their savagery in Ireland having something of the desperation of a man trying to suppress something he fears in himself, they had much to hide. Ireland became the guilty conscience of the English ruling classes, a sort of picture of Dorian Gray on which was recorded their sins and shame, while they turned towards the rest of the world the fair face of English justice.

It was a pork butcher from Belfast who first found a way to drag the picture out into the light and force the English to look at it. His name was Joseph Biggar, and he had been elected by the people of Cavan to represent them in the British Parliament at Westminster.

Until the 19th Century Ireland had been governed through a sort of puppet parliament in Dublin. However, the puppet had had an embarrassing tendency to take on a life of its own, and in 1801 it was bribed, blackmailed and otherwise induced to vote itself out of existence. Those who could not be bribed were assured that the Irish would be much better off as full and equal citizens of the United Kingdom, a promise that was to be remembered with bitterness in Ireland during the Famine.

The amount of actual cash laid out in bribes was over a million pounds, and titles, honors and sinecures were dispensed with equal prodigality. One of the main agents in this market was the Lord High Chancellor of Ireland, the notorious "Black Jack" Fitzgibbon, who had proclaimed that he would make the Irish "as tame as cats." As a judge he was already despised by Irish lawyers, who were not slow to let him know it. In one case he rashly told John Philpott Curran that he could not see any difference between the words *also* and *likewise*. "I venture to disagree, my Lord," said Curran; "the distinction is real. For many years the great Lord Lifford presided over this court. You also preside over it, but not likewise."

His infamous work in Ireland done, Fitzgibbon went eagerly to his reward, a seat in the English House of Lords. He found himself in a larger pool with larger fish, who met his arrogance with withering scorn. "We would not bear this insult from an equal," the Duke of Bedford said coldly, "how much less shall we endure it from the mouth of an upstart and mushroom nobility."

Eaten with mortification, Fitzgibbon returned to Dublin, and died within a year. At his funeral, instead of floral tributes from the still untamed Irish, his tomb was bestrewn with dead cats.

For a long time the Irish members of Parliament were tame enough, being virtually nominees of the landlords. But now democracy was being extended in England, under the pressure of great popular movements like Chartism, led by Irish immigrants among the working class. The widening of the franchise automatically applied in Ireland also, and the introduction of the secret ballot in 1872 was a crippling blow to landlord control. By 1874 there were sixty Irish members of Parliament, all pledged to Home Rule, but arguing among themselves how to get it.

Most of them still pinned their faith to persuasion, but it seemed to Joseph Biggar as a good pork butcher that to sell a customer anything you have to keep him in the store. As it was, the English members simply left the chamber when the Irish tried to put their case. So Biggar decided to keep them there by bringing their own business to a standstill. He started by putting down amendments to every clause of every bill and speaking on each at great length, which he disarmingly called "taking an intelligent interest in English affairs," and soon developed a consistent policy which he expressed in four simple rules:

1. *Work only on government time.*
2. *Aid anyone to spend government time.*
3. *Whenever you see a bill, block it.*
4. *Whenever you see a raw, rub it.*

There was not much sublety about Biggar, and his speeches were not even meant to be interesting. Indeed he would often simply read aloud the longest and dullest government publication he could find, starting with the title and working his way through to the printer's name. Once while he was coming to the end of a particularly massive tome his voice weakened and an Englishman jeered, rashly, that he was inaudible. Biggar brightened up immediately and said that in that case he had better begin all over again, which he did. At one time it looked as if Ireland were going to bore its way to freedom.

His first ally, the young Parnell, saw more clearly the limitations of Biggar's technique, and its potentialities. Being a much cleverer man he was able to devise amendments which made sense and had to be met with reasoned arguments. This gave some justification to his program of obstruction and raised the morale of the Irish members, and they made him their leader. Then he organized them into a disciplined team which, speaking in relays, could delay proceedings almost indefinitely. The climax of his campaign came in January, 1881, when he was able to delay for eleven days the mere presentation of a bill to put down unrest in Ireland. The sitting of January 31st extended to forty-one hours, the longest in the history of the British Parliament, and was ended only by the speaker suspending the Rules of the House, against all its most cherished traditions, and with the ejection of every single Irish member amid scenes of unparalleled confusion.

This turbulent period of British politics produced much drama and eloquence, and also one of the finest impromptu puns ever made. An Irish member was defending as morally justified the taking up of arms by evicted people against the agents of absentee landlords, when he was interrupted by a shout of "Treason!" from an English member. "What is treason in England," said the Irish member, "is reason in Ireland, because of the absentee."

The end of the period of obstruction was just the beginning for Parnell. It had forged for him a weapon, a unified fighting force that would follow his orders unflinchingly, and with which he could make or break English governments. They had nothing to fear themselves in elections, because the Irish electorate would vote for anyone Parnell recommended. In fact at one time discussions were being held with the Indian National Congress about a proposal to elect an Indian for an Irish constituency so that he could speak for Indian independence, in return for Indian support for the Irish movement. Parnell's nominees were elected by majorities like 3069 to 30 (East Kerry) and 4953 to 75 (South Mayo), though Queen Victoria still managed to convince herself they were "low disreputable men who . . . do not genuinely represent the whole country." Furthermore, since the Famine there was a sizable Irish minority in England who voted as Parnell told them, and an Irish Home Rule member was even elected from Liverpool.

In this situation it was only a matter of time before one party or another succumbed to the temptation to seize power with the help of the Irish, and soon Home Rule seemed just an election away. These hopes were destroyed with Parnell by Kathleen O'Shea's husband, but nevertheless for forty years the Irish Question was to remain the central issue of English politics. One party was committed to Home Rule for Ireland, and the other to "killing Home Rule by kindness," and between the two of them the English people were forced to look at what had been done in their name in Ireland, and to make some amends.

I have known English people who have stayed away from Ireland in the same way as a German might be reluctant to visit Israel. But I have seldom heard of any instance of hostility to an Englishman just because he is an Englishman, which is remarkable when one thinks of the attacks on Germans in England during the First World War and other examples of racial persecution elsewhere with far less cause.

The first mention of the English that I know of in Irish literature was a report of a meeting in 1170 when:

The poets and bishops of Ireland were gathered to Armagh, and there they considered what was the cause of the plague of outlanders upon them. This they all understood, that it was because of buying children from the English; for the English, when they were in want of wealth, used to sell their children to the Irish as slaves. And God does not inflict more punishment on him who sells his children than on him who buys them. They therefore counselled that all the English they held in bondage should be let go free. And thus was it done.

However, despite this noble stratagem, the plague of outlanders continued, and they were so common as to be included with animals in Irish proverbs. "Three things to beware of: the horns of a cow, the hoofs of a stallion, the smile of an Englishman."

By Elizabethan times some bitterness had begun to appear:

> *May we never taste of death nor quit this vale of tears*
> *Until we see the Englishry go begging down the years.*
> *Packs on their backs to earn a penny pay*
> *In little leaking boots, as we did in our day.*

But examples of popular prejudice against the English are remarkably few. I have heard a few vaudeville-type jokes, like the one about the Englishwoman asking an Irish butcher for a sheep's head, insisting it must be an English one: the butcher says he has only Irish sheep, but he'll get her an English sheep's head. "Here, Tim, take the brains out of that one." In fact, most of the ethnic jokes told in Ireland are against the Irish themselves, as if through a hospitable desire to reassure the English visitor that his preconceptions about the Irish are correct.

The English misconception that the Irish thought-processes are confused can be traced straight back to one man, Sir Boyle Roche. This old gentleman was a member of the Irish Parliament abolished in 1801 and, single-handed, he led the Irish bull into the china shop of the English language. "Not being a bird," he once said reasonably, "I cannot be in two places at once." Actually, the essential characteristic of his thought processes was that they *were* in two places at once. It was he who originated the famous mixed metaphor, which in its original form read: "Mr. Speaker, I smell a rat: I see him forming in the air and darkening the sky; but I'll nip him in the bud." It was also he who protested against a long-term project with another phrase which has become famous: "Why should we put ourselves out of our way to do anything for posterity, for what has posterity done for us?" At this the House dissolved into helpless laughter and Sir Boyle, fearing he had been misunderstood, begged leave to explain more clearly what he meant, which he did as follows: "By posterity, I did not mean our ancestors, but those who were to come immediately after them." Even this logical explanation did not restore the House to sobriety; indeed it was nearly half an hour before any serious business could be conducted.

On another occasion Sir Boyle referred to revolutionaries as men who would bring the foundation stones of the constitution down around the ears of the nation. Having stunned the House with the horrific prospect of even the law of gravity being defied, he proceeded to an impassioned peroration: "On that very table honourable members might see their own destinies lying in heaps on top of one another. Here perhaps the murderers might break in, cut us to mincemeat and throw our bleeding heads upon that table to stare us in the face!"

Sir Boyle declared that his love for both England and Ireland was so great he "would have the two sisters embrace as one brother," and the picture he conjures up is no more bizarre than the historic relationship between the two countries. One of the few "Irish" stories that says anything valid about Ireland is the old one about the two gunmen lying in ambush to shoot an English landlord, known to be in the habit of passing that way at that time. The victim is late and one gunman says to the other, "I hope nothing's happened to the poor fellow." If this is a true story, and it might very well be, it proves that the Irishman, far from being confused, had a very clear idea of the distinction which should be drawn between an agent of injustice and the same man as a human being. The Irish seem to have the gift of seeing through the Teutonic fallacy that it is possible to make valid generalizations about people, and that these generalizations can then justify persecuting one human being for the failings of another. This idea is unfortunately widely held elsewhere in the world, but it is an utterly silly one, far too romantic and impractical for the realistic Irish mind. He sees people as individual human beings.

It was easy to see the English that way in Ireland, because the country seems to act like a lens that magnifies both good and bad. The English presence in Ireland produced not only the landlord class, but Swift, Sheridan, Goldsmith, Wilde and Shaw. Not only Fitzgibbons but Parnells. And the same disparate influences led as many Irishmen to help build the British Empire as to fight against it. In the days of Britain's greatness one third of her Army and Navy were Irish, and they were led by Irishmen like Wellington, Kitchener, Alexander and Montgomery. Ireland and England have made a lot of history together.

There is a certain type of upper-class Englishman whose movement through the rest of the modern world is accompanied by the faint rushing sound of rising hackles. He converses with his kind in a loud voice in public places, ignoring the natives as he did the servants at home. Subconsciously he feels the cherished conviction, expressed by one of them in 1883, that he "belongs to a race whom God has destined to govern and subdue." Only in Ireland is this almost extinct creature treasured with a sort of amused pity, for the Irish know they created him and then destroyed him.

Ireland was where the English practiced at Empire. It was there they learned the insidious perils of "going native," and developed their protective mechanism of cold aloofness and arrogant reserve. With this equipment they went and founded an empire, dressing for dinner with a stiff upper lip all over the world and finding it all quite easy after Ireland. Meanwhile the Irish were teaching them a harder lesson, that coolness is not enough to keep an empire, and that God could change His mind about their destiny. And finally the Irish taught them how to give up an empire gracefully while they could, and that in the long run respect was more worth having than fear. It was a statesman from the infant Irish Free State who was largely responsible for the Statute of Westminster, the keystone of the modern self-governing Commonwealth. Ireland was the pioneer of all the other emergent countries, and who can guess the amount of bloodshed in India and Africa that her example avoided. In a sense all these young countries are Ireland's foster children as well as England's. A spectator in a divorce court seeing a couple with so many children and so long a life together might think they could not be estranged forever. The shamrock and the rose look well together, and maybe they will yet entwine again.

18. Green Power

Something can be seen from the road between West-post and Castlebar that tells much about modern Ireland. Visible for miles along a green hillside is a series of markings in a deeper green, rather like the phenomenon known in Ireland as fairy rings. But instead of circles, these strange markings spell out, in huge and unmistakeable letters, the words BASIC SLAG.

This is the name of an agricultural fertilizer, and it seems that some energetic salesman must have spent a whole spring day marking out his message in his product. Now the product is advertising itself in a manner that carries instant conviction, a testimonial from Mother Nature herself written in rich dark green grass. It is an example of the medium being the message, which would delight Professor McLuhan. It would also delight anyone who loves the West of Ireland, for such enterprise is evidence that the people of the West, those "wrecks of past racial, religious, agrarian and social storms," as a Royal Commission called them, are moving again.

Indeed one might even have an uneasy feeling that maybe they are going a little too far to use the very grass to project commercials across the face of Ireland. Is the modern Irishman not saying, in the immortal words of Charles Harris, "What's an old birthright compared to a perfectly good mess of pottage?"

Very likely you will find some reassurance around the next corner in the form of a gaily painted gypsy caravan, with a bronzed young couple grinning rather sheepishly at the world over their patient horse. No sooner had these picturesque vehicles disappeared from the roads of Ireland than they appeared again, refurbished and rented by an enterprising firm as a relaxing and congenial way for visitors to see the country and meet the people. Now they can be seen all over the West of Ireland in the summer time, probably with the previous owners in a car and trailer behind them trying to pass.

Tourists are bringing more money into Ireland than any industry, and the Irish realize they do not come to see modern factories, even those performing such remarkable feats as selling sewing machines to the United States, hormones to Soviet Russia, cookers to Afghanistan and musical instruments to Venezuela. Not even new highways with shamrock-leaf interchanges. They want to see the old Ireland, and this birthright has turned out to be a valuable national asset which the Irish have no intention of destroying. In fact quite the reverse. They used to say ruefully that you couldn't eat history, but now it turns out that you can. As a local punster put it, we are proving that we can have archaic and eat it.

First stately homes were converted into luxury hotels, where the visitor could live the life of a country gentleman, apparently the secret ambition of every Western European male. Next came the restoration of old castles like Bunratty, where the visitor is entertained like a mediaeval nobleman. Both these places offer a dream come momentarily true, but the latest development offers something with deeper psychological significance, an opportunity almost to commune with the very soul of Ireland. More prosaically, I suppose one might call it the Restoration of the Unstately Home. A company informatively calling itself Rent-an-Irish-Cottage is building in tiny villages in the scenic West a number of new old-fashioned thatched and whitewashed cottages especially for renting to visitors. They will look exactly like the traditional Irish cabin, and inside there will be the stone floor and the open hearth for the turf fire and everything just like in the old days, but there will also be modern plumbing and an electric kitchen.

I read somewhere else that a plastic thatch has been developed, and no doubt that will come in useful. At which point, if not before, I suppose someone will cry out in horror at this little gray fake in the West. But if a man of Irish descent comes back to the old country to live there for a while in make-believe that his ancestors never left it, there is nothing false about using the conveniences they would have chosen if they could. This idealized Irish cottage is a sort of amend made by the present to the past, as well as an exile's dream.

This charming and probably very profitable idea was conceived by Brendan O'Regan of the Shannon Development Company and is being financed partly by the local communities (who stand to benefit enormously, financially and otherwise) and partly by the Irish Tourist Board—in Irish, *An Bord Failte*, the Board of Welcome. This is an organization for which I am acquiring such vast respect that I believe if there was a similar one in Hell the Christian churches would be out of business. I am even beginning to suspect they were behind a mystery which has been puzzling me for twenty years, the Strange Affair of the Erudite Road-menders.

Up until a dozen or so years ago, the roads in the West

of Ireland seemed to be festooned with men sitting by the side of the road chipping stones and drinking tea out of battered billycans. One peculiarity about them was that the road was always worse after they had finished, for all they did was convert every pothole into a little mountain of flints, so that you had not only broken springs to fear but punctured tires. The other peculiarity was their conversation, at least what I overheard of it on this occasion. One of them said, "But that was *after* the War of the Austrian Succession."

All I know about the War of the Austrian Succession is that it involved the Empress Maria Theresa, and although her field marshal was one Ulysses Brown from County Galway I doubt if it had much influence on Irish history. Yet here were these road-menders bandying it about like last Sunday's hurling result. Now I'm beginning to suspect that they were an early effort by the Tourist Board, inspired by the story of the Women of Mungret. Hidden somewhere in the Great Bog of Allen were a secret government clothing factory turning out the picturesque uniform of greasy brown cloth and string, a little steel mill fabricating billycans battered into the traditional shape, and a little training college from which a steady stream of qualified road-menders, primed with folklore and quaint sayings, were released onto the roads of Ireland to reinforce Ireland's reputation as a land of learning and take the place of expensive direction signs.

On this theory even their strange craft made sense. Ireland is a small country which, if suddenly planted down in the Gulf of Mexico, would scarcely even qualify as a menace to navigation. American tourists are tempted to tear around it between breakfast and lunch, and then go on to spend their money elsewhere. We are stuck with this small country, the Tourist Board must have reasoned, so we shall simply have to spin it out. Some judiciously placed stones would either make the visitor slow down or spend several nights in a hotel while new springs are flown out from Detroit.

Nowadays, of course, all the roads are smooth and the old road-menders have been paid off. The visiting motorist finds everything he is used to, except traffic, and is enticed into exploring the countryside more fully by excellent signs. Only occasionally do these signs let him down, by being in Irish only. *Telefon* is not hard to translate, and even *Aer Phort* is not too baffling, but some of the others can confuse visitors. "If *Oifig an Phuist* doesn't mean *Gentlemen*," Charles Harris said on his first visit to Dublin, "I did a very silly thing in the post office this morning."

The case for reviving the Irish language is almost entirely emotional, though Sean O'Faolain for one claims that Irishmen cannot express themselves properly in any other tongue—an argument he advances in movingly eloquent English. The only people I ever heard of who put it to any practical use were the Irish UN troops in the Congo, who found it a valuable security aid, and Brendan Behan in a pub when he was besieged by English reporters for an interview. He consented to give one, but in Irish, and the reporters had to pay his drinking companion to act as interpreter. But despite valiant efforts such as this the fact that Irish is a compulsory subject in schools is violently resented by many parents on the grounds that it is making their children "illiterate in two languages," and they are now enrolling themselves in a Language Freedom Movement.

In 1955, in an attempt to encourage the use of Irish in the legislature, the Committee on Procedure issued an English-Irish phrasebook containing 150 useful remarks for politicians, such as "Talk sense," "That is not the answer to my question," and "What about the election pledges?"; and I am afraid many deputies have found it quite sufficient for their needs. There are of course exceptions:

Mr. Dillon: *The Deputy finds it hard to get the wheel of his intelligence around the axle of my argument. I cannot blame him. You cannot put a wheel designed for more modest purposes around a substantial axle.*

But generally the debates lack the fire and brilliance that used to be displayed by the Irish members in the British Parliament. Partly this is because they are now required to conduct the humdrum business of government, but it may also be because the natural leaders of the country were mostly killed in the 1916 Rising and in the civil war which followed the birth of the infant Free State, or were driven out of politics by disillusionment.

The most remarkable fact about the 1916 Rebellion was that it was pointless from a material point of view, and indeed this entire period of Irish history must be the despair of those historians who believe that mankind is activated by economic forces. As a result of the movement started by Parnell the Irish now held possession of their land, the country was progressing constitutionally to very much the same degree of independence it was eventually to attain, and the great majority of the people were quite well satisfied with this state of affairs. Then, at the same season Patrick had confronted the Druids and Brian Boru had defeated the Norsemen at Clontarf, a few young idealists occupied Dublin Post Office and read to the bemused passersby a proclamation that seemed to come from a forgotten world.

Irishmen And Irishwomen: In the name of God and of the dead generations from which she receives her old tradition of nationhood, Ireland, through us, summons her children to her flag and strikes for her freedom. . . .

For a few hundred men to challenge the whole British Empire in the middle of a world war had been, of course, just a form of ritual suicide, like the self-immolation of Buddhist monks in Vietnam. But as day after day in their plodding way the English executed the leaders, wounded and all, they made burning patriots of thousands of other young Irishmen and set the whole country alight. A terrible beauty had been born, as Yeats put it, and it led all Ireland out of the normal course of History.

The world in which the Irish found themselves after 1916 was more like that of religion than of politics, in that men were fighting for their vision of Ireland rather than for any immediately attainable material objective. But it is the tendency of all religious movements to become first schismatic, then institutional and finally hypocritical, since there is no way of assessing the truth of their claims. De Valera himself recognized this when he said: "In England you can say anything as long as you do the right thing; in Ireland you can do anything as long as you say the right thing."

The schism in the patriotic movement, between those

who accepted the settlement with England and those who rejected it, became institutionalized into the two main parties which still exist today. The party system in the Republic of Ireland is therefore much more like the one in America than anything else in Europe, and it has permitted a refreshingly pragmatic approach to many problems. Ireland has had fewer socialists than any other European democracy, and more state enterprises than most. It has also produced governmental decisions of an astounding maturity for a nation with the history of Ireland. The design of its coinage, for example, was made the subject of an international competition under the supervision of W. B. Yeats, and the drawings of an English artist accepted. The first president of the country was a Protestant, and the pro-English minority was treated with so much consideration that even now they hold far more of the wealth of the country than is justified by their numbers.

While accepting the Protestant minority community as good Irishmen, a trust which they fully justified, the government worked at removing other traces of the English. Everything official was painted green, and although the embossed initials of British monarchs can still be discerned on mail boxes, someone must have made a fortune out of green paint. Kingstown became Dun Laoghaire again, and Queenstown Cobh. People were encouraged to change their names back to an Irish form, Sullivan becoming Suilleabhain and O'Kelly O Ceallaigh. Even the Norsemen were not quite forgiven, a not altogether successful attempt being made to change the Scandinavian name Dublin to the original Irish name of Baile atha Cliath. More practically, rich estates in the fertile east were bought and parceled out to farmers from the barren west, whose ancestors had been "migrated" more forcibly centuries ago.

But there were no revolutionary reforms, and in many ways the new governments were more conservative than the British administration would have been. The decline of the countryside went on, the young people continued to emigrate, the birth rate fell and the gay colors of the Gaelic revival seemed to have been trodden into the mud of the civil war. The new nation seemed to have become a "grocers' republic," a land of celibates and dullards stagnating behind a curtain of clerical black.

To the outside world the most noticeable odor from this cultural backwater was produced by the censors, who provided a classic illustration of the precept that there is no defense except stupidity against the impact of a new idea. To be fair to the Irish people, censorship was sold to them originally as a defense against the English Sunday newspapers, which brought the prurient news of the half-world into 350,000 innocent Irish homes; the British Government itself eventually took action against them by prohibiting the publication of divorce court evidence. Many people in Ireland accepted the censorship as a necessary protection for Irish culture, and had no idea that it would be used for its destruction.

It should have been obvious from the attitude of some of the advocates of censorship that they would not be satisfied with banning a few tabloid newspapers:

At present the spiritualised Irishman is quickly passing away, and all the brute that is in him is being fed almost to the point of moral leprosy, to be followed by a tempest of fire from heaven.

This calamity was narrowly averted by the banning of books by such evil-minded foreigners as Aldous Huxley, H. G. Wells, Graham Greene, Daphne du Maurier, Pamela Frankau, Somerset Maugham, Warwick Deeping, Kingsley Amis, Balzac, C. S. Forester, Andre Gide, Maxim Gorki, Noel Coward, A. J. Cronin, Bertrand Russell, Arthur Koestler, Mary McCarthy, George Orwell, Margaret Mead, Beverley Nichols, Marcel Proust, Thomas Mann, Anatole France, Georges Simenon, Ernest Hemingway, Dylan Thomas, Sinclair Lewis, Thomas Wolfe, John Steinbeck, William Faulkner. Erskine Caldwell, Upton Sinclair, Tennessee Williams, Françoise Sagan, Hugh Walpole, Evelyn Waugh, Laurence Durrell, Compton Mackenzie, Andre Malraux and Muriel Spark.

It proved to be little protection for an author to be a Catholic, and still less for him to be an Irishman. The works of no less than forty-four Irish authors were banned, these moral lepers including Bernard Shaw, Oliver St. John Gogarty, James Joyce, Samuel Beckett, Iris Murdoch, Liam O'Flaherty, John O'Hara, Brendan Behan, Edna O'Brien, Kate O'Brien, Maura Laverty, Frank O'Connor, Sean O'Faolain, L. A. G. Strong, Joyce Cary, George Moore, Sean O'Casey and Robert Graves.

The Censorship Board had become a redoubt of the type of Catholic who seems to think the Pope is soft on sin, and it proved very difficult to dislodge them. Irish writers, however, notably Sean O'Faolain, carried on a valiant guerilla action, and in 1956 the government disabled the Board by infiltrating onto it two of its opponents. These infuriated the chairman by not only refusing to ban new books, but allowing the sale of omnibus volumes containing books already banned, an attitude for which they had no justification but good sense, but which the government tacitly approved. The chairman resigned, followed by his supporters, and the Board was thankfully reconstituted with more reasonable men. Since then censorship in the Republic has been moderate, as censorships go, and five thousand books have been released from prohibition including most of those by Irish authors. So ended a second and mercifully short Dark Age, in which Britain and Europe nurtured the culture of Ireland as she had once done for theirs.

From one point of view the period between 1920 and 1960 could be regarded as one in which Ireland retreated into a *cul de sac,* letting the rest of the world pass it by. But from another it could be thought of as an essential period of stability, during which the country retired into a cave to lick its wounds, heal its scars, cure its fever, and take stock of its situation. It began to emerge into the light with the premiership of Sean Lemass, who, symbolically enough, had been too young to actually fight in the 1916 Rebellion and had been released by the authorities with a kick on the behind. With the success of his government's first Five Year Plan the country began to look to the future rather than the past.

From a growing and prosperous Dublin, now housing nearly a quarter of the population, and once again a European capital, new ideas began to erode peasant conservatism. New industries, tourism and television helped to reduce the paralyzing boredom of life in rural Ireland, which clerical puritanism and depopulation had made into the sort of place which justified Sidney Smith's description of the countryside as "a kind of healthy grave."

Nowadays it seems that Howard Johnson country begins at Limerick. The West seems to be jumping straight from the 18th Century into the Twentieth, reminding one of those central Asian tribesmen who take the aeroplane for granted but are startled by the bicycle. There are modern motels and diners where before there was nothing, and domestically the people have proceeded from oil lamps to electricity and from no plumbing at all to modern bathrooms. The new hotels have huge bars with cabarets, providing social centers where the young people of the district can gather and where they mingle with the tourists. The young people have also generated a particularly Irish type of pop music phenomenon known as the Show Band, which has taken the place of the old wandering minstrels. These young musicians, all clean-limbed and short-haired, provide as their name implies a complete evening's entertainment consisting of a mixture of traditional type Irish ballads and pop tunes played in dance tempo. At any one moment the Irish Top Ten will include both, and conversely there have been counterattacks by Irish music on the folk song salient, with a success that is hardly surprising in view of what has been referred to as the "strange and startling richness" of Irish folk music.

Irish television, competing with British television over much of the country, is projecting startling new ideas into the darkness of rural Ireland. For the conservative countryman it is a window on the world like Keats's magic casements which, you will remember, opened on perilous seas in faery lands forlorn.

An interesting peculiarity of Irish television, by the way, is that companies avoid the interview/testimonial type of commercial, having found that they are met with complete incredulity. It seems that the Irish appreciate only the soft sell.

Signs of new energy are to be seen all over the country. A Tidy Towns Competition, run by that Tourist Board, has brought about dramatic improvements in the appearance of at least 531 Irish towns and villages. That was the number who entered in 1968, when the winner was Rathvilly, County Carlow. The ordinary Irish people seem to have found a new pride in their country and new hope for its future.

Some people believe that what did most to restore the self-confidence of Ireland was the emotion-charged visit of President Kennedy in 1963, probably the happiest and most hopeful event in Irish history since his ancestor defeated the Norsemen at Clontarf in 1014. A woman journalist, thinking of the time it had taken for the free air of America to produce a president from the poor Irish, described him as "the Irishman of the year 2000." Kennedy not only embodied the hopes of Ireland, but found the words to express them:

The Ireland of 1963, one of the youngest of nations and the oldest of civilizations, has discovered that the achievement of nationhood is not an end, but a beginning. In the years since independence you have undergone a new, peaceful revolution, an economic and industrial revolution, transforming the face of this land, while still holding to your spiritual and cultural values. You have modernized your economy, harnessed your rivers, diversified your industry, liberalized your trade, electrified your farms, accelerated your rate of growth and improved the living standards of your people. . . . Other nations in the world in whom Ireland has long invested her people and her children are now investing their capital as

212

*well as their vacations in Ireland. . . . This revolution
is not yet over.*

19. Dark and True and Tender is the North

The American authoress Mrs. T. P. O'Connor asserted
that she could "invariably tell by looking at people
whether they like gravy." With similar percipience some
Ulster Protestants claim they can recognize Roman Catholics by sight. A girl in Donaghadee told Brendan Behan
to his face that she did it "from their wee button noses,"
oblivious to the fact that by her standards Brendan must
have been one of the Exclusive Brethren.

Some people have seen more subtle differences between Ulster Protestants and their Catholic compatriots.
Reporting on them in 1809 Sir Jonah Barrington found
the Protestant population of Ulster to be:

*a people materially differing in character from the
aboriginal inhabitants—particularly sharp witted, fond
of reform and not hostile to equality, prone to intol-
erance without being absolutely intolerant and disposed to republicanism without being absolutely
republicans. Of Scottish origin, they partake of many
of the peculiarities of that hardy people. Harsh
minded, perservering, selfish, frugal . . . as brave,
though less impetuous than the western or southern
Irish, they are more invariably formidable. Less*

213

> *slaves to their passions than to their interest, their habits are generally temperate; their address quaint, blunt and ungracious; their dialect harsh and disagreeable; their persons hardy and vigorous.*

Many people would still agree with this assessment, subject to some minor exceptions. The Ulster dialect varies widely, even between one part of Belfast and another, and is often far from harsh, seldom disagreeable and often poetically expressive. *Blunt* is a more appropriate word than *ungracious* for their address: a shop assistant in Belfast may ask "Are ye gittin'?" instead of "Can I help you?" but she will go to as much trouble to help you as her counterpart in Dublin, and is perhaps more likely to get you what you want. And of course Ulster Protestants are not nowadays "disposed to republicanism," a fact which is the wonder and despair of other Irishmen.

The thoughts of those other Irishmen are inclined to turn to the unmarked grave in a Protestant cemetery in Dublin of Robert Emmet, who asked that his epitaph not be written until his country had taken her place among the nations of the Earth. It has not been written yet, and Kathleen ni Houlihan must regain the last and richest of her Four Green Fields before the soul of Robert Emmet can rest in peace. The defection of Ulster was to most Irishmen a national tragedy and disgrace, explicable only on the assumption that the people of Northern Ireland had been temporarily misled by bigotry and greed into betraying their country's past.

Not surprisingly the situation looked rather different from north of the border. From there it seemed rather as if the people of the South had been misled by gunmen into betraying their country's future. Ulstermen would agree that much wrong has been done in Ireland, having fought English injustice themselves in Ireland and America as valiantly as any; but they would also say that the duty of Irishmen is to the future of their country rather than its past; and that in the modern world that future must lie in association with Britain.

This fact has loomed large in the smoky air of Belfast, Ireland's only industrialized region. Here in the Black North are grouped the Irish linen industry, the biggest shipyard, ropeworks, tobacco and carpet factories in Europe, and a conglomeration of other industries dependent on the British market. Emotionally this feeling of dependence on England is reinforced by the stockade mentality of the Protestant minority, who for centuries have feared for their religion and livelihood if they were given over to a Catholic government representing the descendants of those whom their ancestors dispossessed.

This mental state was described by one Southern Irishman as a settled hallucination accompanied by annual brainstorms: the latter being the fervent 12th July celebrations of the Battle of the Boyne, a river that is remembered more religiously than the Alamo. Indeed it is said that one visitor who asked what the procession was all about was told to go home and read his Bible. One has only to see this procession to know what makes Ulster tick, and why the tick is sometimes reminiscent of a bomb; and yet also why the colorful spectacle is enjoyed by so many Catholics and broadcast on Republic of Ireland television. In Belfast the procession takes hours to pass and is full of music ranging from patriotic Irish airs (all of which, of course, have two sets of words) to pop tunes, played by flute bands, accordion bands, brass bands and pipe bands both Scottish and Irish, while children dance happily along the sidewalk. Missing nowadays are the huge Lambeg drums, which were more like artillery than music, but were said to be capable of the most subtle rhythmic and tonal effects in the hands of masters. They were played with thin canes, and in the old days there were drumming contests that lasted for hours, the contestants' knuckles dripping with blood. They were usually accompanied by a single inaudible flute, apparently on the theory that in law this converted the din from an offensive noise into a musical performance.

To make up for these sinister but fascinating drums we now have mini-skirted drum majorettes and girl musicians, but visitors looking at the gorgeous silk banners depicting Old Testament scenes, Victorian statesmen, English monarchs and obscure Protestant theologians are inclined to feel that this procession lost its way somewhere back in history and is no longer quite sure where it is going.

The Assembly of Ulstermen in 1782 in Dungannon proclaimed that "As men and as Irishmen, as Christians and as Protestants, we rejoice in the relaxation of the penal laws against our Roman Catholic fellow subjects." Yet only a few years later Ulstermen felt it necessary to found the Orange Order to safeguard their "civil and religious liberty," a liberty for which they proved they would defy any power on Earth, including the British throne.

At times during the variegated history of the Orange Order its love of liberty has been expressed in a bluff and forthright opposition to the Catholic Church. The old

Orange toast, nowadays gleefully recounted by amused Catholics, used to be:

> *Here's to the pious and immortal memory of King Billy, who saved us from knaves and knavery, slaves and slavery, Popes and Popery, brass money and wooden shoes. And if any man among us refuse to rise to this toast, may he be slammed, crammed and jammed into the barrel of the Great Gun of Athlone. And may the gun be fired into the Pope's belly, and the Pope into the Devil's belly, and the Devil into the roasting pit of Hell, and may the doors of Hell be banged shut and the key kept in the pocket of a brave Orange boy. And may there never lack a good Protestant to kick hell out of a Papish. And here's a fart for the Bishop of Cork.*

No one seems to know why the Bishop of Cork warranted such airy dismissal, and part of the toast is contrary to the requirement of an Orangeman to "abstain from any uncharitable words, actions or sentiments towards his Roman Catholic brethren"; and indeed contrary to the general obligation of the Order not to admit "persons of an intolerant spirit." Circumstances have at times made it difficult for Ulster Protestants to maintain the essential distinction, generally so well understood in Ireland, between ideas and the people who hold them. Love and concern for fellow human beings as victims of error has too often been driven out by fear lest, through those same human beings, error should prevail.

The growth of the power of the Catholic Church in Ireland in the 19th Century alarmed Protestants, and the proclamation of the doctrine of Papal Infallibility in

1870 and the hounding of Parnell did nothing to reassure them that it was growing any less arrogant and intolerant with the passage of time. The rebels in 1916, making heroes of themselves in Dublin, made fools of the quarter of a million Irishmen fighting equally valiantly with the British Army in France, whose relatives and friends felt a bitter sense of betrayal. Hostility between Loyalist Protestant and Nationalist Catholic hardened into a cold war which was to last for a generation.

Looking back, it may be that the first breach in the partition was made by the Luftwaffe. In April, 1941, Ireland was partly at war and partly at peace. Dublin was brilliantly lit, well-fed and thronging with Germans. Belfast was blacked out, rationed and as totally at war as London, except that she had not yet been bombed. The experts had calculated she was too far away to need defending. The Luftwaffe did not agree, and one night rained on the unprepared city the heaviest concentration of high explosive bombs dropped on any city in the United Kingdom in the entire war, followed by ninety thousand incendiaries. The news that Belfast was in flames reached Dublin in the early hours of that morning, and the government of that carefully neutral country did a remarkable thing. They ordered out the Fire Brigades. Every fire engine between Dundalk and Dublin raced north and before dawn they were crossing the suddenly meaningless frontier, their headlights blazing through the blacked-out villages of County Down towards the burning capital of their old enemies. Between them Irishmen from both sides of history put out the fires of Belfast, and next afternoon the tired firemen went quietly home, unthanked. Unthanked officially, that is, because a neutral country would not do that sort of thing, and officially nothing had happened. Something had though, not in the newspapers and the speeches of politicians, but perhaps in the hearts of the people. Like so many crucial events in the history of Ireland, it had happened at Easter.

The visit of the Dublin firemen became part of the rich folklore of Belfast, with all the other stories of the Blitz. Like the man who told his wife, standing in the street shaking her fist at the Luftwaffe, to "come in and stop aggravating them." Or about the couple who were fleeing for safety to the hills when the wife wanted to go back for her false teeth and was told by her husband, "Come on, woman. It's not ham sandwiches they're dropping." A man, returning to consciousness to see the insignia of the Dun Laoghaire Fire Brigade, is said to have marveled at the power of a bomb that could hurtle him over a hundred miles. In fact the whole country had been blown considerably nearer to the middle of the 20th Century.

So when the new young Prime Ministers of North and South, Terence O'Neill and Sean Lemass, presiding over the youngest cabinets in Europe, dared to meet one another in friendly talks on cooperation, Irishmen on both sides of the border applauded this supreme act of leadership. The only opposition came from the benighted Protestant sectarians whom a Presbyterian Liberal, the Reverend Albert McElroy, described as frosty-faced Pharises with self-issued tickets to Heaven; and from the hoodlums whom they, foreswearing violence themselves, led within a stone's throw of their opponents. The government put down Protestant terrorism with the same firmness it had used to deal with the IRA, and Protestant public opinion repudiated their extremists as the Catholics had repudiated theirs.

Welcoming this new spirit, the dynamic Minister of Commerce in the Northern Government, Brian Faulkner, made the generous admission that "in repudiating the actions and words of the extremists and in talking of efforts to improve relationships within the community, we are being tacitly forced into endorsing the criticism of our predecessors and of Unionist policies and allegations of unfair treatment towards the Nationalist minority." For their part, the Nationalist politicians admitted with equal frankness that they had been wrong in refusing to cooperate in the running of the country, but the distrust engendered by their previous attitude could not be dispelled overnight and they complain not always with justification of continued discrimination against the Catholic minority. Speaking in the Northern Ireland House of Commons in January, 1968, the Minister of Home Affairs, a forceful young law reformer called William Craig, assured them with evident sincerity that he understood their concern, and himself called for practical action by every citizen to bridge the division in the community:

A distressful past has left us with a deep wound, but one which is rapidly healing. . . . We have come a long way in these past few years, and I think that the public would like to have not only less discrimination, but less talk of discrimination: less revival of old antagonisms and more trust in each other and confidence in our future.

Confidence is one thing which Northern Ireland still

lacks, and for no very obvious reason. The province is as beautiful as anywhere in Ireland, and as devoid of natural resources, so its great industries were built on nothing but the hard work and enterprise of the people. Under the leadership of Terence O'Neill it is blossoming with new factories, schools, universities, even with whole new towns linked by exquisitely designed modern freeways. The level of wages is fifty percent higher than in the Republic. Its government has shown more initiative and efficiency than the rest of the United Kingdom in many fields and is regarded as a model by the advocates of regional self-government for Scotland and Wales. And, most important of all, it is now offering to the world the all too rare spectacle of a governing race voluntarily surrendering its privileges. And yet there clings about it a curious atmosphere of self-doubt and vulnerability, almost of guilt.

Writing about West Berlin, a journalist in the *Sunday Times* commented that it was the only country in the world where you see people running to take up reserved seats in aeroplanes. He ascribed it to a feeling of insecurity; a panic fear of disorder, of the unexpected, perhaps even of freedom itself. It is interesting that people do this in Northern Ireland too. Even if it's only because they are not used to flying and want to get a seat by the window so that they can see out, it still has some symbolic significance. The country has taken off, is now moving at a great speed, and the people are not quite sure where they are.

They have a great deal of history to leave behind. In the case of the Catholic community the problem is the same as that of underprivileged people the world over. It is a little sad, but not strange, that an Ulster Catholic mother wiping her child's dirty face should say, "Now, that's more Protestant looking." The situation of the Protestant majority is rather more complex. They have just begun to realize that some of their history is discreditable, and that all of it started abruptly about 350 years ago (a mere yesterday in Irish terms); and they have not yet been able to bring themselves to accept as theirs the earlier heritage of the rest of Ireland.

By a fateful coincidence the very name of Terence O'Neill may lead them out of their wilderness. This is probably the greatest name in Irish history, stretching back through the great Ulster chieftains who fought the English for centuries to King Niall of the Nine Hostages, who brought St. Patrick to Ireland; and it is almost eerie to see an O'Neill in today's Ulster Parliament facing a distinguished Opposition spokesman who bears the name of Roderick O'Connor, the last king of Celtic Ireland. When Ulster Protestants relegate to their proper place the recent unhappy memories of sectarian animosity, and accept the greater heritage that the historic name of O'Neill represents—and perhaps even the great liberal traditions of the Protestant and Anglo-Irish Ireland of Swift, Curran, Tone, Emmet, Parnell and Yeats and before them Cuchulain and the other heroes of the rich Ulster legends—they will have a mythology and a history more proud than any in the world, even those of the Southern Irish.

Brendan Behan, a Catholic, a Dubliner and a member of the IRA, believed that the future of Ireland lay among the working people of Belfast, and he may very well have been right. The Ulster Protestant may contribute as much as he did in America to the making of the

Irishman of the Year 2000, the new Irishman foreseen by the Ulster poet George Russell as an amalgam of all the peoples who have found their home in Ireland:

> *One river born from many streams*
> *Rolls in one blaze of blinding light.*